THE EXTREME IMPROV BIG BOOK OF IMPROV GAMES

DAVID PUSTANSKY

The Extreme Improv Big Book of Improv Games by David Pustansky

Published by Extreme Improv

www.extremeimprov.co.uk

First published in 2020

All artwork by David Pustansky

Paperback ISBN: 978-1-8381326-0-6

Ebook ISBN: 978-1-8381326-1-3

10 9 8 7 6 5 4 3 2 1

First Edition

JOIN THE EXTREME IMPROV COMMUNITY

Extreme Improv welcomes you to join our continually growing community.

Website: www.extremeimprov.co.uk

Facebook: www.facebook.com/extremeimprov

YouTube: www.youtube.com/extremeimprov

Twitch: www.twitch.tv/extremeimprov

Twitter: www.twitter.com/extremeimprov

Instagram: www.instagram.com/extremeimprov

TikTok: www.tiktok.com/@extremeimprov

Snapchat: www.snapchat.com/add/extremeimprov

Extreme Improv Podcast Network

Podcasts available on all major podcast platforms

- Extreme Improv Podcast
- Extreme Improv Radio Rumble
- Extreme Improv Chat Show
- Extreme Improv Skills Show
- Jet Lagged and Loving It Travel Podcast
- Superkick Mania Pro Wrestling Podcast
- Mega Movie Podcast
- Games Monster Podcast

Table of Contents

I: INTRODUCTION

Welcome to the Extreme Improv Big Book of Improv Games! In this book you'll find dozens and dozens of fun to play improv comedy games that are sure to bring a smile on your face and a healthy dose of wackiness to any show, rehearsal, work place, classroom or random Thursday evening that you choose to play them on!

I've written this book with the hope that it is both accessible to newcomers to the world of improv comedy, whilst also being in depth enough that more experienced performers will find new games and insights in how to improvise successfully.

Many of the games featured in this book are original creations I've developed for the Extreme Improv Comedy Show which I produce. These are either completely new games which I've created from scratch, or classic games I've put 'extreme twists' on to give them a fresh lick of paint. I look forward to seeing players and groups all around the world try out these new games, just as I have enjoyed playing games I learned from TV shows such as Whose Line Is It Anyway?, radio programmes like Just a Minute, and the many improv shows I've seen throughout my life in theatres.

As well as my own creations, I've included dozens of classic improv games I'm sure many of the seasoned improvisers out there will know and love. With these I've tried to include tips and insights which may help put a new perspective of how to play them the next time you're on stage.

If you're like me, you'll have just skipped past this part of the book and started flicking through the many games to see which ones you know, and which ones are new to you. As a heads up for those of you who did start reading here, there may be some acting or improv specific terms or ideas in the book which you may not have come across, but for the most part I've attempted to keep things in everyday language. This book isn't intended to teach you how to act or improvise completely from scratch, and there are certainly some more tricky games listed (we are called Extreme Improv after all), but I hope that the multitude of tips and thoughts included will help everyone to become a more confident performer.

If you still haven't skipped to the list of games, the next few pages will give you an overview of what you're in for, and what both improv and Extreme Improv are. I'll also tell you a little of who I am, and why you should consider listening to me rattle on about the hopping rule and why it's worth stitching together a two headed T-shirt!

So, without further ado, get ready as you are about to enter the world of Extreme Improv...Good luck!

II: WHAT IS IMPROV?

If you're brand new to improvised theatre, it is basically a performance which isn't scripted or rehearsed. That isn't to say it's not practised though...

Improvised theatre is usually classified into two main categories: 'Short Form' and 'Long Form'. More people are familiar with short form, but it is actually the more complicated to explain.

Long form improv can most easily be explained as an improvised play or musical. If I said nothing more here, I'd have given you a good idea of what to expect from long form improv.

Long form can have lots of variations just as plays, musicals and films can, but generally speaking a long form show will be a play or musical which is improvised from start to finish, and which follows one storyline and group of characters. The other main variation of a long form show is a collection of scenes that are connected in some way – either with a continuing theme or that one scene inspires the next.

In long form, the inspiration for the story/theme of the show is usually suggested by the audience at the beginning, and very often that is the end of interaction with the audience. It's very possible with long form shows that if an audience member came in late and didn't witness the audience suggestion, they wouldn't know the show was improvised.

This book focusses on short form improv which can most easily be explained as a sketch show that is completely improvised. This however doesn't quite explain it enough, and that's why my usual go to when someone asks me what Extreme Improv is, I'll answer 'It's a bit like Whose Line Is It Anyway?'

The TV show Whose Line Is It Anyway? Is the most widely known example of improv as it has been on television all over the world for decades. Because of this show, people are more familiar with short form improv, but if you're not familiar with Whose Line, this is where explaining short form gets more complicated.

The sketches in a short form show are most commonly referred to as games. This is because a short form show is not just a collection of mostly unrelated scenes as you would find in a normal sketch show. Instead, each scene is set up with a selection of rules which the performers have to abide to. These rules can vary in a game, from characters only being allowed to speak in questions to characters not being able to use a specific body part.

A short form show will usually have continual audience interaction and one or more performers may take on the duties of a host in order to ask the audience for suggestions for each game. They will also explain each challenge that the performers are about to undertake.

Every improv game has its own rules and flow, and in this book, I will cover over 100 games. Some of these are covered in more detail than others, and this is because there is a lot of cross over between the skills required for each game. So the advice I've put in one section may also apply in another section.

It's also worth noting that I've written this book based on my own personal experiences performing, directing, and teaching improv shows, and just because I have found the advice I give in this book works for me and people I've worked with, it may not work 100% of the time for you. Improv is not a one size fits all thing. It is perfectly ok if upon reading this book you're inspired to try things differently. You may even find that doing exactly the opposite to what I suggest is what works for you. In either case, if I have helped you form your own ideas and build your own toolbox of improv skills and games I'm happy to have been part of the process.

Broadly speaking there is no right or wrong in improv, but I would say there are choices you can make that will either be more successful or less successful. Improv and art in general are subjective, but in this book as much as possible I try to help you to understand the concepts and logic behind the games, their rules and the things you can do in each challenge to play it successfully.

If you believe a man can fly, so will your audience.

III: ABOUT THE AUTHOR

My name is David Pustansky. I'm a British born actor, director, filmmaker and writer and at one time or another I have been involved with many different areas of the performing arts and film industries. This has included acting in films and on stage, producing hand drawn animated films, recording and releasing songs, designing sets and props, presenting on red carpets, writing and performing sketch and stand-up comedy and teaching performing arts to people from age 3 years to well into their 80s.

Some will say I'm scatter brained, or have lacked career focus to have tried my hand at so many different creative endeavours, whilst others will say I'm a typical Gemini or impatient to not stick at one thing and continually juggle different pursuits.

I would say I'm just stupidly fascinated by creativity and have a constant thirst to learn new skills and understand different types of art forms. Does this mean I'm the perpetual Jack of all trades and master of none? Yes. Definitely. But I also believe that having a broad understanding of many different creative arts makes you better at them individually.

Which brings me back to improv. When performing improv, you are acting. But in addition to acting you are also your own script writer choosing the words you say, and you're your own director guiding you to make the most dramatic, funny or emotional choices, whilst also making sure the audience can always see and hear you most clearly. Because I have pursued many different creative projects, I feel it has made me a better improviser as I have an understanding of how these various aspects all need to come together.

I was born in London but lived a lot of my life in Buckinghamshire. I trained professionally as an actor at a drama school in London, and it was there where I decided to start organising some after school improv sessions...until I was told I wasn't allowed and banned from doing improv outside of lessons...before we'd even been going a week.

Apparently as I had already got a few years improv experience it was decided by the powers that be, that if I organised these sessions it would be jumping ahead of what they were teaching at the school. This is a story for another day, but I can say that being given a big fat 'no' rather than being encouraged with a traditional improv 'yes and' to practice and rehearse in my own time with friends did give me the determination to continue on an undeniable path of improv. And this directly led me to create what is today known as Extreme Improv.

Improv has been a big part of my life for years. Like so many other people out there have done, I've written up my personal bucket list, and in one way or another improv has helped me fulfil lots of them.

- Be in an improv show... Check.
- Start an improv theatre company... Check
- Make some hilarious friends... Check...they're improvisers.
- Check if you should write 'check' or 'tick' on your bucket list...apparently tick if you're English...
- Travel abroad. Tick...and usually to do improv.
- Do improv in outer space...working on it...
- Start a podcast. Tick...it's about improv.
- Perform improv underwater... Tick.
- Write a book...hello!

IV: ABOUT EXTREME IMPROV

Extreme Improv has performed live shows at theatres, comedy clubs and festivals all around the world. We have played all over the UK and played in several states in America from California to Florida to Alaska and more in between. We've taken Extreme Improv to Tokyo, and all over Europe, and have welcomed performers from all over the world to join the show and guest with us.

Extreme Improv has expanded greatly beyond live shows and workshops to include regular video series, podcasts, streaming virtual shows, and lots more beyond. That's where things are at the time of writing, but to give a brief history of the company, we do have to jump back in time to when I was still at drama school...

During the summer holidays whilst still at drama school I put together 'The ImProDigies Theatre Company' as it was originally known, and I arranged for our debut show at The Etcetera Theatre in London.

Whilst attending drama school, I wasn't technically supposed to do any shows outside the drama school while the course was happening...but equally the summer holidays aren't technically while the course was happening. Some think I organised this show just to rebel against my being banned from doing improv outside the lessons, but realistically I just missed doing improv and wanted to do it more.

The first show we did was called 'It's A Scandal!' and it was a few short form games followed by an improvised play, all of which were based on actual news headlines of the day. The show was a success and also played in a festival that summer before I had to put the ImProDigies on hold for a year whilst I finished training at drama school.

In the years that followed this, there were lots more shows here and there, and this included times where there were less shows as I focussed on other non-improv projects. Each time I'd put on a new improv show, I'd create new formats which included shows that focused on themes like the news of the day, people's relationships and hang ups, and science fiction. Every run of shows would have a new name and format created from scratch...that is until I created Extreme Improv.

So why is it called Extreme Improv? What makes it extreme?

These are common questions I get, and if you are wondering if it means we perform on the rooves of burning buildings whilst our legs are chained together...no, it's nothing that dangerous. Maybe one day, but not thus far.

Originally planned as a one-off idea for a show at the Camden Comedy Club in London, I created what was then known as Extreme Championship Improv. The name was a riff on Extreme Championship Wrestling, and just as ECW was seen as more dare devil version of the WWE wrestling, where things were tougher and more gritty, I wanted Extreme Championship Improv to be a more challenging and daring version of a short form improv show. I'd also borrow the competitiveness and heightened drama from wrestling along with the idea that the winner earns a championship belt.

And sure enough, for the show I got a custom championship belt for the champion to pose and brag with. It was only after the initial shows when performers were showing off their championship victories on social media and getting dozens of likes and shares as if they'd won an Oscar that I realised that maybe Extreme Improv shouldn't just be a one off show.

Now competitive improv is not a new thing, and nor is the parallel to professional wrestling, but in most instances other competitive improv shows are team based whereas Extreme Improv is mostly based around the idea of there being a solo champion.

The Championship and competition are just smoke and mirrors. Winning and losing games really does not matter in Extreme Improv. The goal I teach performers is not to win as the focus, but to make the show fun and entertaining for the audience. Winning is just a bonus treat.

Competition aside, I have also been on a mission with Extreme Improv to invent innovative new improv games that haven't been played before. Or to create new versions of classic games where there are 'extreme twists' to make the games more challenging and to subvert the audience's expectations.

Innovative new games, tougher versions of classic games and the heightened OTT emphasis that goes with the chase to become Extreme Improv Champion. These are what I tell people makes Extreme Improv 'extreme'. So sorry if there are no burning buildings whilst escaping from shark tanks with straightjackets on...we'll do a show like that one day...

And if you're wondering why we dropped the word 'championship' from the title? It's simple...Twitter. Championship has twelve letters in it and made tweeting about upcoming shows tricky with Twitter's limited character count. Those extra twelve letters could mean the difference between fitting in info about an upcoming show and running out of...

So that briefly explains where Extreme Improv came from. As for where it's going? It's going to be an exciting journey to find out! And a journey I hope you will all join us on. We've taken our brand of improv from small comedy venues in London to bigger stages on other continents. We've expanded from just the stage to video series and audio versions of the show, to the interactive virtual online Extreme Improv XStreamed shows which allow players and audiences from all over the planet to play and laugh together.

I can't say where Extreme Improv will end up next, but my hopes are for it to always continue moving forward. To explore strange new venues. To seek out new improvisers and new platforms to improvise on. To boldly go where no improv show has gone before!

V: SOME GENERAL TIPS

Here's a few general tips for successful improvising. These are some general guidelines that should apply to any and all of the games in this book and beyond to long form improv.

#1: Yes, and... Probably the most well-known concept in performing improv. The idea of 'yes, and' is that if another performer gives you an offer of an idea in a scene you should say 'Yes, and...' to accept their idea and then add onto it with an idea of your own. Let's look at an example:

Player 1: Shall we go to the beach?

Player 2: No.

In this example Player 1 gave Player 2 the offer of going to the beach, and Player 2 blocks the idea, which means that all of the potential of the scene where the characters go to the beach is lost. Sure the scene can continue, but it can only continue by finding a new storyline, or by taking the time needed for the players to circle back round to once again deciding to go to the beach. Here's what can happen if you say 'yes, and'

Player 1: Shall we go to the beach?

Player 2: Yes, and when we get there we can search for buried treasure!

As you can see, within just two lines the characters now have an entire scene full of potential laid out in front of them.

The concept of 'Yes, and' doesn't mean you can't ever say no, which is what some often take this rule to mean. For example, if a character said:

Player 1: Can I kill you?

Player 2: Yes, and then I'll be dead!

You can see how this may be problematic for the scene, as most characters would want to protect their own lives. Here's an alternative look at how this exchange could go:

Player 1: Can I kill you?

Player 2: No, because if you do you'll never find where I buried the treasure.

As you can see, Player 2 said no, but was still able to make an offer to continue the scene whilst staying true to their character's instinct to live.

The point of 'yes, and' isn't that you literally have to say yes to everything, but rather that you shouldn't block ideas given to you. In most instances it will always work better to accept and embrace an offer rather than to block an idea.

#2: Listen, listen, listen! When improvising you have no idea what the other performers are going to do, so make a big point of always listening to everything going on around you. Listen to the rules for games that you are about to play. Listen to your scene partner so you know and understand what they are contributing to the scene. Listen to the audience so you can learn from their reaction what things do or don't work.

#3: Don't talk about something...do something! A very common mistake I see improvisers make is to be given a scenario and then have the characters talk about it rather than do it.

For example, if your scene is about going on a road trip, don't spend the entire time of the scene talking about 'where should we go?' Just get in the car and start driving! And what's more – arrive at places! The Grand Canyon, the Eifel Tower, Big Ben – you could have a scene take you to all of these places in the same time as someone else has a scene where they still haven't got in the car yet. It doesn't mean that either scene will be better or worse than the other, but if the audience have been promised a scene about a road trip, give the people what they want!

As one more example of this - if the scenario you have been given is to make up a scene about Star Wars, don't make the first line you say be 'did you see the new Star Wars movie at the cinema?' By doing this you're instantly telling the audience that instead of this being a scene set on the Death Star with potential for force powers and light sabres...this is a scene about nerds reviewing a movie. Don't talk about Star Wars...give them Star Wars!

#4: Value your audience: If you are performing in front of an audience who have taken the time to support your show, do your best to reward that support with the best show you can give them. Treat them with respect, build a rapport with them and send them home happy. If you engage with your audience and give them a fun and entertaining time, there's a good chance they'll come and support you again or recommend you to friends and family.

If you do a show and there's a small audience, make sure you don't punish the people who have turned out to see you by phoning it in or giving them a lesser show. A smaller audience is an opportunity for a more personal show especially for them!

Also avoid in-jokes between performers or jokes that call back to a previous show as these will exclude audience members not in on the joke.

#5: Have each other's backs: Look after your scene partners, and your scene partners will look after you. Whatever the situation is, if something isn't going well, trust your fellow performers to help you out and get you through the scene, and do the same for them. Many improv games are presented as competitive, but realistically you're always a team. In those moments where you or your teammates need support be there for each other.

#6: Don't talk over each other: You may have a great idea but share the stage time. If your scene partner is talking find your moment to interject. And if you're talking and they interject, allow them the floor. By sharing the scene, you'll all end up with plenty of stage time.

#7: Put the focus on your scene partner: Building off the last tip, here's a really clever way to ensure everyone gets a fair and equal level of stage time. Endow your scene partners with important attributes in the scene.

Let's say your scene is about people on a plane which will crash as the pilot has had a heart attack. You could say 'Don't worry I will save the day as I am the flying doctor and will land this plane and save the pilot's life!' However, by saying this you put all of the importance in the scene on yourself, and effectively cast yourself as the main character.

As an alternative approach, you could say to your scene partner 'Didn't you used to take flying lessons when we were at medical school?' An offer like this establishes that your scene partner has the skills to land the plane, while also establishing that both you and your scene partner could potentially solve the medical issue. This approach shares the important roles in the scene and gives everyone something to do.

You could be even more selfless and say, 'Didn't you used to take flying lessons while you were at medical school?' This will give all the important roles in the scene to your scene partner. You may think this excludes yourself from the scene, but it doesn't. As you were the player endowing your scene partner you have already ensured you have had dialogue and set up the entire scene. If you continue endowing your scene partner in this way, you will be continually contributing to the scene, and will help ensure both players are featured throughout.

That isn't to say that you should always endow your scene partner and put the focus and responsibility on them at your own expense. As with anything, it's about finding balance. I'd suggest that the ideal would be that both you and your scene partner endow and put the focus on each other equally. For example:

Player 1: Didn't you take flying lessons while you were at medical school?

Player 2: That's right. But I'll need your help to land this thing while I perform CPR on the pilot. If I instruct you, can you take control of the plane?

As you can see from this example, Player 1 endowed Player 2 with all the importance in the scene with this opening offer. Player 2 then accepted the offer, and gives an offer of their own back to Player 1. This means that both characters are now of equal importance in the scene. By putting the focus on each other both players end up with equal stage time and things to do in the scene.

#8: Don't stand directly in front of another performer: This is basic stage craft, but a very easy mistake to make for non performers. If you stand directly in front of another performer, the audience will not be able to see them. If you stand directly in front of another performer and face them, the audience will not be able to see either of you.

#9: Don't put your back to the audience: To expand on the last point, as a general rule try not to put your back to the audience, and especially whilst talking. The audience won't be able to hear you well, as your voice will be travelling away from them. Also, so much of the story telling we do as actors is on our faces. People read each other's emotions from their expressions and body language. There may be times when putting your back to the audience could be effective, but this should always be a conscious choice of yours to create an effect by doing this rather than you just have your back to the audience because you haven't thought about it.

#10: Respect other performers and your audience: People of all backgrounds and life circumstances can enjoy improv. Improv shows, auditions and rehearsals should always feel a safe space for the performers and audience members. Help maintain a safe, positive and inclusive environment that is welcoming to everyone by treating each other with the same level of respect and support that you would want to be treated with yourself.

Be sensitive with the characters and the content of the scenes you make up. Humour is often drawn from misfortune, mishaps, clichés, and stereotypes, and whilst it's ok to explore themes and can be funny to push boundaries, there is a fine line between having fun and making fun. Be cautious when making references to people from different countries, religions, ethnicities, genders, sexualities, ages, or disabilities. Engage in open discussions about what is and isn't acceptable from your shows and players, learn from mistakes and lead by example.

The respect we show each other also extends to personal space. Improv scenes aren't rehearsed. And often you may find yourself working in a scene with someone you don't know well. Don't make assumptions that because the audience suggested your characters are husband and wife that you can kiss the other performer. Likewise if you're told that you're both playing boxers don't assume it's then OK to punch another performer, and especially not because 'that's what my character would do.' Well intentioned or not, that excuse doesn't fly.

No one should be made to feel uncomfortable, or at risk of injury whilst performing. Improv requires a lot of trust that you are always in safe hands with your scene partner, and everyone in the company. Trust can take months or years to build and can be very easily broken.

#11: Don't direct your fellow performers: Some people are more extrovert or dominant personalities than others, whilst some are more introvert or shy. If you're a more outgoing improviser be mindful that it can be easy to lead the direction of the scene you are in at the expense of the other performers being able to contribute. Of course there are times when someone can and should take the lead in a scene, but if you have this ability put it to considerate use to help facilitate other less confident players to enable their ideas rather than just push your own. A shared stage is a happy stage.

#12: Winning doesn't matter: It really doesn't. A lot of the games in this book are designed that they can be played competitively, and if you wanted to you could play to win every time. But a lot of the time playing to win won't benefit your show. As far as things go with Extreme Improv, I always teach and direct players that the main purpose of performing in a show is to give the audience a fun and entertaining time. Making the show enjoyable is the aim, not winning.

Winning is nice but sometimes winning in a technical sense makes things less entertaining. You'll also find that if you win lots people will at first be impressed, but very quickly they'll just want someone else to beat you. Audiences love to route for the underdog, so whilst it's great to win...if you win too much the audience will turn on you!

Don't take games too seriously, and if you can get a laugh over winning a game, I'd often say that getting a laugh is more valuable to make the show entertaining. And if your aim is to have fun rather than win you're more likely to have fun...which means you win either way!

#13: Embrace failure: One of the most important rules in the entire book. Failure is your friend. Audiences love outtakes and blooper reels from films and TV shows. If you've ever been to a recording of a sitcom you may have noticed that when an actor messes up their lines the audience might laugh louder and longer then when the actor said the line correctly.

When an audience is at an improv show they are aware that what they are watching is made up on the spot. Part of the enjoyment of watching improv is just watching performers attempt something. If you do something 'right', great – the audience will like what you did, but if you do something 'wrong', awesome, there is still a very good chance they'll like it. The audience will understand that you attempted to do something that you were making up on the spot, and will appreciate your efforts. In this sense 'going wrong' is still going right!

Win, lose or draw, you can always make the best out of a situation in improv if you embrace failure. Once you understand this principal, it can be one of your greatest tools as an improviser.

If something goes wrong – you mess up, forget a character's name, go off key in a song or whatever, just embrace it! This can mean saying something to acknowledge the mistake, laughing at yourself, or attempting whatever went wrong again in hops for a better result. In these cases always acknowledge the mistake with a smile and enjoyment and the audience will enjoy that you're not taking yourself too seriously.

Alternatively, you can just confidently continue as if the mistake was your original intention. Sometimes that can be styling something out to smoothly cover a mistake, or it can be acting as if a mispronounced word is a real word which you continue to say incorrectly. Either way, the audience will almost certainly realise you said/did something you didn't intend to, but will enjoy your embracing the mistake and building off of it.

On the flip side, if you don't embrace mistakes, mishaps and errors, you are at risk of becoming an awkward turtle. And no one likes an awkward turtle.

If you act awkward because you're not sure what to do, feel you've done something 'wrong', start apologising, make excuses or blame others you'll feel awkward. But worse than that, you'll project your awkwardness onto the audience, and they'll feel awkward.

So, if you don't understand a game, or make a mistake, I would suggest that you should loudly and proudly admit that you don't know what you're doing. Embrace the failure! The audience will probably find this funny and they'll be on your side to get it right. The Emcee will probably think it's ok to explain what you haven't understood once more, and if you still don't understand...give it a go anyway! The joke will become that you haven't understood what you're doing and within a couple of minutes it'll all be over anyway.

#14: Make big and bold character choices: Short form is just that – short! You don't always have oodles of time to create nuanced characters with intricate backstories. In a short form show you may find that you play 10 or 20 different characters within an hour. Each of these characters should feel unique. To achieve this, try making some bold choices in terms of voice, physicality, attitude, emotion etc, to keep each character feeling distinct. That doesn't mean everything has to be big and loud, as a character could be introvert, creep about and whisper just as much as stamp about and shout.

#15: Reincorporation: You may have heard the term 'a running gag' which means a joke that comes up multiple times. You probably know a bunch of different catchphrases from characters on TV. You might have seen a film where events at the end mirror events from the beginning, or ideas that tie back to things that have happened before. These are all examples of reincorporation, which is a very useful tool in improvising.

If you do an action, say a phrase or make a joke within a show, you may find that you will get a laugh or positive reaction from the audience by repeating the same idea later on in the same show. The audience will recognise what you have said, make the connection to what happened earlier, and they will enjoy it as a result. Sometimes you may even find that the joke becomes funnier the second or third time.

A word of caution is to not milk a joke too far. If you go to the well one too many times you may find that you no longer get a laugh if you have killed the joke by repeating it to death. Similarly, be careful not to do a call back to a joke from a previous show that your audience may not have seen. Unless the joke is funny again in its own right, it probably won't work as well.

#16: Have fun! My personal golden rule is to do all I can to make a show fun for the audience. If they enjoy it, you'll probably enjoy it... and if you enjoy it, they'll probably enjoy it too! Laughter is contagious, and people warm to positivity. Doing improv, telling stories, playing and pretending to be other people and saying silly things is fun! Don't take things too seriously and just enjoy yourself!

VI: EMCEE/HOST/PRESENTER

Most short form improv shows have an Emcee/host of some kind. For the purposes of this book I will mostly refer to this role as the Emcee. The responsibilities of an improv show Emcee are to:

- Welcome and warm up the audience.
- Introduce improv games and explain their rules.
- Ask the audience for suggestions or 'gets' (as they are often called) for what the performers will improvise about.
- End the improv games and segue onto the next challenge, often making humorous comments and observations along the way.
- Act as timekeeper for improv challenges that are time based.
- To ask the audience to vote for winners and losers on challenges where applicable.

Do you need a host?

The short answer is yes, but how you choose to do this has a few options as there can be a few ways to approach having an Emcee.

#1: The Dedicated Emcee

This is the Emcee whose only role within the show is to introduce the improv challenges, ask the audience for suggestions and such like. A dedicated Emcee won't participate in any of the improv challenges themselves, and with this they will serve as a neutral facilitator who enables the other performers to take part in scenes.

#2: The Player-Emcee

A performer who fulfils all or most of the duties of the Emcee, but also takes part in the improv games. A Player-Emcee will come under more scrutiny than the other players as they have more "power." So remember what Spider-Man says here and that is that with great power comes great responsibility. As Player-Emcee you can choose to be harsher on others then on yourself to give yourself an unfair advantage. Be warned though that this may paint you as a bad guy to the audience which can be fun to play, but if not handled correctly may not benefit your show.

#3: Shared Emcee Role

This is where more than one player shares the responsibilities to Emcee the show. One or more performers may welcome the audience and warm them up, and then take turns to introduce the various improv games. There is still the chance that players could twist rules to their advantage, but keep in mind that the other players could do the same when it is their turn to introduce a game.

There is the comedic opportunity when sharing the Emcee duties that players taking turns can put each other in tricky scenarios. Remember though that if you all do this too much you'll spoil the fun for everyone. Moderation is key here.

VII: WHAT KIND OF EMCEE ARE YOU?

The Friendly Emcee

This approach is where your demeanour is bright, happy and positive and you use these qualities to project a happy and supportive atmosphere onto the audience.

You encourage the performers to do well and are complimentary regardless of how things have gone in the games. Win, lose or draw you say well done for trying!

The Dark Side

This type of Emcee will still be friendly and likeable to the audience but is also willing to be harsher on the players and stricter with the rules.

This version of an Emcee is the one dishing out the difficult challenges to the performers and giving mildly sarcastic and amusing remarks that may joke about the efforts of the players. The purpose of this type of host isn't to be mean to the performers, but rather to help get the audience on the performers' side. This is based on the logic that the players are the underdogs having to overcome tough challenges set by a harsher Emcee.

Decide if your hosting style is nice or mean.

VIII: WHERE CAN THESE GAMES BE PLAYED?

One of the great things about improv is that you can do it almost anywhere. For the most part all you need is your imagination. The games in this book are written primarily with the stage in mind but can be played in a variety of settings. In this section I'll briefly go over the most common settings where you could play these games. I'll also say a few thoughts on how you may have to modify the games to work in these settings.

STAGE/WORKSHOPS

Traditionally speaking, most improv shows happen on stage. There will be a live audience who will give suggestions and create a social and community feel to the atmosphere which is one of the biggest strengths to performing on stage.

Usually the stage will be empty except for some chairs that the performers can use in scenes, or to sit on between scenes if they're not in a game. The Emcee may have a chair or sometimes a desk to one side, and if you have a pianist accompanying you, they may also be off to one side.

All the games in this book are suitable to play on stage as they are described.

If you're using the games in theatre workshops you should be able to play them exactly as you would if it were a show. Use other participants as audience members to give suggestions and feedback.

FILM

OK, so you aren't likely to go to the cinema and see a movie of improv games (although some films have been heavily improvised) but there have been TV programmes based on improv shows.

It is also possible with cameras and editing software becoming ever cheaper and more accessible, that even the smallest of improv groups could adapt their shows to be filmed and edited with a television style presentation.

If you're acting for film rather than stage, you'll find that you can play with your performance levels. On stage people usually give a more heightened performance, with projected voices and a more physical and visual style. Techniques for acting on film can often be a lot smaller with close ups to catch subtle changes in emotion. Shots can then be edited together in post-production from many takes, which isn't possible on stage.

Improvising for screen is somewhere between acting for stage and normal acting for film. Whilst you will still be performing in one take like on stage, you won't need to play things as heightened, or project your voice to the back of the room in the same way. And whilst it's usual for any improvisation based TV show to have a studio audience as you would for a stage show, they are there to provide the atmosphere, but are not your primary audience in this instance.

The big thing to keep in mind is that even though you may have a live audience at the recording, the audience watching the recording at home are your main audience in this setting. This means you'll have to have camera awareness to make sure you're playing to the camera and microphones. So this means that really funny idea you have to run to the back of the audience and continue the scene from there may not work if the cameras are not set up to capture it, and if you're not lit back there. Entertain the studio audience, but not at the expense of the audience who would be watching you on screen.

Most games in this book should be able to be played on film exactly as they're described, but as a performer you could experiment with playing to the camera and what the camera can/cannot see. There are some technical based games which use green screens or specific camera angles, and cannot be easily replicated on stage, but they are not featured in this book.

WORKPLACE

It is more popular than ever to have improv as part of team building days and social events at places of work. The places of work could be anything, and not even remotely be related to performing. Often improv companies will offer improv sessions as a service, where one or more facilitators come into a place of work and lead an afternoon or day of improv.

These can help with team building, problem solving, general socialising and much more. These events will often feature exercises where the focus is on the experience for the participants and are not as suited to be played in front of an audience.

In terms of adapting the games in this book, most of them can be played as exercises in groups/pairs with no audience, just for the participants to experience and enjoy. And naturally they can be played in front of the other participants if you set up a performance area and an audience area. This would be like them hosting their own mini improv show.

A word of warning is that it's very common for adults to be a lot more shy than children when it comes to performing, so if they're reserved and slow to warm to the games do what you can to make everyone feel at ease. Plan your sessions well and note that many of the games in this book are designed to be challenging for the Extreme Improv Comedy Show.

As a facilitator it's your role to make everyone feel valued and included, and you can start with easy games as ice breakers to warm less confident people into it. Pick games that will suit the level of the participants, and if you feel they are responding well and can cope with a more 'extreme' game you can always throw one in as a 'real challenge'.

IN EDUCATION

School, college, university, and weekend drama clubs are all great places to play the games in this book. Whether they are used in specific drama lessons, improv societies at uni, or just as warm up exercises for normal school lessons there are a ton of games in this book that would work well.

Most can be played exactly as they would be on stage, but there are a few things to be aware of. As with other sections, I'll mention that some games are designed to be tricky, and you'll have to judge the level of the students you are teaching a game to.

An observation I have made is that younger children can often have fantastic imaginations but may struggle with rules of games and pushing the story in a scene forward. My advice here would be to start with easy games and to promote the idea of making sure that scenes have a beginning, middle and end.

Older children often get self-conscious of performing in front of peers in case they are judged. So even though they will understand the rules better, you may find that there is a resistance to performing. My advice here would again be to start with easy games so they can shake off their inhibitions and get used to performing in front of each other.

AUDIO

Shows like Just a Minute, and Sorry I Haven't a Clue have been around for decades, and even Whose Line Is It Anyway? got its start as a radio show. Improv on radio has been around a long time, but with podcasts and internet radio being much newer inventions it is now easier than ever to produce an audio version of an improv show.

It is easy for inexperienced performers to forget that the most important audience member in an audio improv show is the microphone. Or more specifically the audience who will later be listening to the show and can only hear it if you use your microphone properly. I've seen players give great performances where they turn away from the mic, or scream into it. Both should be avoided.

Many of the games in this book will work well for an audio-based performance, but not all. Also some of the games that can work on audio will need big modifications. Visual and physical based games simply cannot be played successfully over audio. And games that have multiple players in the scene at once will require discipline to make sure the performers don't all speak over each other.

On the plus side, the audio format lends itself to players playing multiple parts if they can change their voices/accents. You can also do tense and intimate scenes where you whisper in the listener's ear through the mic. And in terms of world building it's easier than ever to allow the audience to imagine you're fighting a dragon in their mind's eye if all they can do is hear you. If you're on stage wrestling around with a folding chair and calling it a dragon, the visual can sometimes limit the audience's imaginations.

VIRTUAL SHOWS

I'll flat out acknowledge that I'm writing this book in the year 2020 and in the middle of lockdown during the COVID-19 pandemic. Why is this relevant to write? Because a year ago I would have had almost no idea what a 'virtual improv show' was.

This pandemic has meant that the improv community has had to use its own skill to adapt to what it is given in the moment and come up with a way to continue whilst theatres are closed.

If there hadn't been this virus it's unlikely that virtual theatre would have become a thing which it now has, and this may be one tiny sliver of a silver lining within all the tragedy of these times. Does it replace traditional theatre? Not at all, but it is likely that in the future this format of improv shows will continue, and in time will only get better and better as the technology improves.

I'll avoid talking too much about the technology requirements of virtual improv as this will probably be outdated even by the time I've finished writing this book, but here's a general overview of virtual improv...or at least how we did virtual improv back in the day (if you're reading this in the future.)

Virtual shows will use video conferencing software to allow performers to see and hear each other over the internet. If this software is combined with some kind of broadcasting software it will allow a show to be broadcast out to members of the public via platforms like YouTube, Twitch or Facebook.

Extreme Improv XStreamed is the name of our virtual streaming show, and I started developing it from the first week of lockdown in the UK. As this format is still brand new, here are my current findings for those considering creating a streaming improv show.

- All games that work in an audio format will work on a virtual show, and have the added benefit that your performers can be seen.
- Some games that work on stage, but not on audio will work on a stream. These may require modifications, but you may find some do not work at all. These will often be more physical based games, because with the current technology it's not possible for players to walk across stage, interact physically or exchange non mimed props.
- You also have the added benefit that you can now have players in different countries play together and people from around the world can all watch at the same time.

- Audience participation is currently mostly limited to being able to suggest things, give feedback and engage with you via text chat and comment sections.
- It is possible to have audience join via audio, but this is problematic currently. On a stage you will naturally have the focus of the room, but if your audience is joined to a streaming show via sound only, their sound will come across equally to your own. This may overlap and distort what the performers are doing. There may be workarounds to reduce their level, but nothing at the time of writing seems ideal.
- Also, if you find you have a heckler join via audio you could find they intentionally disrupt the show. Most video conferencing platforms will give you controls to remove someone, but that is if you can identify who the troublemaker may be.
- Specific benefits when performing streaming shows compared to live shows include that it is easier than ever to add audio and video to a show, and that you can use built in green screen technology to create virtual sets. You can also add filters to performers faces.

Future editions of this book will update this section with new information. So, if you're reading this many years after 2020 congratulations you quite probably have a first edition!

Performing improv online creates new challenges, but also gives new possibilities.

IX: INVENTING NEW IMPROV GAMES

One of the things I'm most proud of that I've done with Extreme Improv is invent a bunch of new improv games. Truth be told I spend an unhealthy amount of time trying to devise new games. I've invented a few dozen new improv games, and many of the new games I've invented are in this book. I love introducing new games to players and audiences, and I'm excited to think that more people will get a chance to play them as a result of compiling this book together.

This said, I'm aware that it's very possible that during the stone age, two cave men on different continents could have both 'invented fire.' Completely independently from one another. In this sense I'm certain that there are games in this book which I'm sure I invented but have also been devised in a similar or even the exact same way by someone else who are also certain that they invented it. The only way to know for sure would be for someone to track down the first evidence of a game being played, which is easier said than done. With more and more shows being recorded, newer games should be easier to track, but even that doesn't account for games devised and played in rehearsals and classrooms.

I'd like to think that I've created over a third of the games I've included in this book, and that a bunch more are games where I've put new spins on old classics.

I'd also encourage anyone reading this to try to create new games as well, as it's always fun to throw a new idea in a show or rehearsal.

Putting New Spins on Classic Games

Games I've put new spins on include the many versions of an Alphabet Scene you'll read about in the coming pages. A few years ago, I was playing an Alphabet Scene and I got confused and started going backwards through the alphabet to letters we'd already gone past. This caused some hilarity as I and my scene partner got increasingly confused, but it got me thinking...can this game go backwards? How about a Reverse Alphabet Scene?

Now an Alphabet Scene that goes backwards seems almost too obvious for it to be my creation. I'm sure it must have been done before somewhere. I've not come across anyone else playing it in my travels, and many people I've introduced it to have told me they haven't seen it before.

So regardless of whether it was my invention or not, it did get me questioning how could I take this idea further for other new spins?

It's never made sense to me that as children we learn the alphabet going ABC, and then as soon as we use computers or typewriters the alphabet goes QWE. It can be tricky for some to learn to type but once you have, the order of the letters as found on keyboards is what most people interact with far more than your ABCs. So, what if players were tasked with learning the QWERTY alphabet? What if there was a QWERTY alphabet game as the ultimate challenge?!

From here I started thinking about other alphabets. Russian maybe? Possibly, but I assessed that that is too difficult for English speaking players. NATO Phonetic alphabet? Greek alphabet? But how would they work?...I know, what if you have to say the names of the letters (Alpha, Bravo etc) to start each line, instead of just the letter they represent? Boom! Two new games.

This is an example of my thought process for how I developed these new games. This process can sometimes take months or years before I spot a new possibility for a game. But what if you want to develop brand new games from scratch that aren't a spin on an existing game?

Creating new games from scratch:

Here is my thought process which led to a few more creations.

When trying to come up with new games I will often try to think of a feature that can be focussed on. This can include things like features of language, or physicality.

One day I was writing a poem and it included alliteration, which is where the same letter or sound comes in quick succession and is pleasing to the listener's ear. An example would be something like 'The Doctor dared to dream of dating the Dalek'.

I had tried to develop a game previously where you could only say words beginning with a specific letter, but players found it too hard. The restriction was too limiting.

But then I thought 'What if instead of this being a restriction that you could only say words beginning with one letter, it was a goal?' That you can say words beginning with any letter, but that you have the goal to make as many words as possible all start with the same letter. From this the idea for the game Alliteration Anarchy was born. But this game would also lead to several more.

I wondered what the opposite or reverse of this would be? And can it be a game? What if you're not allowed to begin any consecutive words with the same letter? There are 26 letters, so that may be too easy for the performers to be worth it.

I drew a blank on this idea, but it got me thinking on the goal aspect of the game. What if there was a similar game, but instead of having the goal of using letters and words, the goal was focussed on physicality. What if instead of being assigned a letter of the alphabet you were assigned a body part? And the audience would vote who they felt made the best creative use of it in the scene? That is how I came up with the concept of the game Body Language.

From there I once again applied my 'can I reverse this' filter to create another new game. Fortunately, I found that I could. What if this time you're assigned a body part that you're not allowed to use at all? This was the basis of creating the game Immobilise.

X: HOW TO USE THIS GUIDE

Below you will see an example of how the games are laid out in this book. You will see the various headings followed by an explanation of what information you will find in that section.

EXAMPLE GAME NAME

Emcee Intro Script: The Emcee Intro Script is an example script of what the Emcee could say before each game.

In theory any performer should be able to understand how to play a game simply from the rules read out by the Emcee before a game. In reality the Emcee's introduction of a game is designed primarily for the audience's benefit, and not the performers. To master most games there will be more rules and tips to follow than what the audience need to know.

For a performer to fully understand a game please read the rules section of each game which will give more detail on how to play.

Challenge Style: This will explain the type of challenge each game is – scene based, monologue, song etc.

Players: This will explain how many players can play each game.

Ask the audience for: This will give examples of what the Emcee should ask the audience for suggestions of so that the players have the starting point for their scenes.

Setup: If there are special requirements needed for a game such as a chair, microphone or prop these will be listed here. If all you need is an empty stage and your imagination, the Set Up heading may not be listed.

How to play the game: This section may seem like it's repeating the Emcee Intro Script, but whereas the focus of that section is to explain the rules of the game to the audience, this section is a more complete explanation of how a game works so that a performer can understand its objectives and progression.

Some improv games have definite rules. Some have clear objectives. Many have steps to playing the game successfully which aren't quite correctly explained by either term. The rules and objectives in this section will break down the steps to playing a game into numbered points, but please note that the steps do not always have to be made in the order they are listed.

How does the game end? Here I will explain how the game being played could be brought to a conclusion. This could be a judgement call made by the Emcee that the scene has reached a natural conclusion or run out of steam. It could be a time limit, an error made by a player causing them to be eliminated from the game, or a goal achieved by a player meaning the game ends as they have won.

Pro Tips: The Pro Tips section is to give some extra tricks of the trade to help you go from being a good player of a game to a great player of a game.

A note about rules, modifications and variations:

In this book I have written that some games can be played with time limits, or where players have a certain number of lives, or get eliminated if played in teams. I've written these ideas for certain games where we at Extreme Improv will often play the games this way, but that doesn't mean you have to play with time limits or lives etc.

Games where I haven't listed these rules could still be played this way, and likewise games where I have listed teams or timers could be played without them.

As you practice games, play around with these elements and experiment with what works best for you. Modifying games can increase or decrease their challenge and I'd encourage you to be open to trying games tweaked in different ways as you may discover a new way to play that I've not listed.

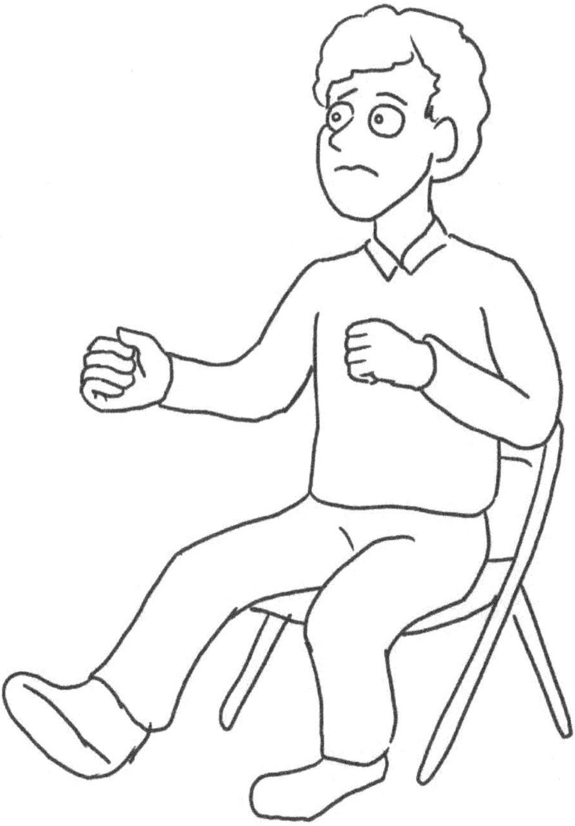

Start your engines!

XI: THE LIST OF GAMES

So, this is the real reason you're here! Training is over! Or to wage a guess you skipped all the previous pages just to get to the games. Good choice! Those pages were mostly filler anyway.

You want to know the games that the Extreme Improv team play in the shows, and here you will find a bucket load of them, along with dozens of bonus games that are common in the world of improv.

Let the games begin!

Roooooaaarrrr!

SECTION 1: WATCH YOUR LANGUAGE

The games in this opening section all focus on features of language, and play with restrictions and conditions we can apply to how we speak. This includes the number of words you're allowed to say and the types of words and sentences you can use to communicate.

1: SINGLE SYLLABLE SHOWDOWN

Emcee Intro Script: This game is called Single Syllable Showdown. There will be two players in the scene at any one time. Whilst performing the scene the players are only allowed to speak in single syllable words. So for example, they can say 'hi' but they cannot say 'hello'. They can say 'Dave', but they cannot say 'David'.

If a player says any words that have more than one syllable, that player will be eliminated and replaced in the scene. If a player hesitates for too long without speaking, they will be eliminated from the scene. And if a player speaks in what we call a circular conversation – that is a conversation that keeps repeating the same words and doesn't move the story on....they will be eliminated from the scene. Whichever player is left at the end wins the game.

Challenge Style: Scene based/Language challenge

Players: 2+

1 vs 1 (With each player having 5 lives)

Teams of up to 5 vs 5 (each player has one life)

Note: There are only two active players at any one time. Teams of up five vs five can compete in an elimination style, but there will only be two players competing actively in the scene.

Ask the audience for:

A scenario such as a place of work.

Setup: Any players not actively in the scene stand in the wings/on a back line waiting to enter the scene when it is their turn. If a player is eliminated, they leave the playing space and return to the wings/back line.

How to play the game

#1: Single syllable words only! The players have the restriction that in the scene you can only say words of one syllable.

For example: You can say 'Hi' but you cannot say 'Hello'. Or you can say 'Dave' but you cannot say David.

If a player says any words that have more than one syllable they will either lose a life (1 vs 1) or be eliminated from the scene, and replaced with a new performer.

#2: Hesitation Rule: If a player hesitates for an extended period of time without speaking, they lose a life or are eliminated from the game. This rule prevents performers claiming they were having a dramatic pause to buy themselves time.

#3: Circular Conversation Rule: A player will lose a life if they use the same words or phrases over and over again. Doing so doesn't move the scene on and will become boring to watch. Always keep the story moving forward by using a wide variety of different words.

How does the game end?

If you are playing 1 vs 1 where each player has a certain number of mistakes they can make, the game will end when one player runs out of lives.

If you are playing as a team based game, the game will end when all players on one team have been eliminated by making mistakes and there is a winning team left with one or more players who have not been defeated.

If you are playing where players aren't eliminated for mistakes or that previously eliminated players re-enter the game in a round robin fashion, the game can either end after a time limit or the Emcee's discretion.

Pro Tip #1: Keep good pace! The audience will think this game is easy if you take your time and speak slowly. You will impress them more if you leave very few gaps in your speech. This doesn't mean you should speak so rapidly that people can't understand you.

Further on this idea avoid the pitfalls of scenarios such as a scene set in space or underwater. For some reason players performing these scenarios often speak very drawn out and slowly, which makes the game easier to achieve and less fun for the audience as the challenge is lost.

Pro Tip #2: Have fun with the words you use! 'sposed' is a shortened form of supposed, 'peeps' is a shortened form of people and 'bout' can be used in place of 'about' as three examples. If you use commonly shortened versions of words the audience will find this tactic clever and funny.

What doesn't work though is if you use shortened versions of words that are never normally shortened. Such as saying 'I went to the hosp' instead of saying hospital. You may get a laugh once or twice, but quickly the audience will feel you are cheating in the game.

2: NUMBER OF WORDS

Emcee Intro Script: The next game is Number of Words. In this game the performers will create a scene, but they are each going to be assigned a number of words they have to say each time they speak. So, if a character has the number 5 it means every sentence they say has to be exactly 5 words long. No more, no less.

Challenge Style: Scene based

Players: 3-5

Ask the audience for:

#1: A scenario such as a dangerous situation you need to escape from.

#2: A number to be assigned to each player. This will dictate how many words they must say in each line of dialogue. It's usually sensible to have the number of words be between 1-5, but you may be able to push this to slightly more.

How to play the game:

#1: The players creating the scene have to speak their lines of dialogue with the exact number of words per line as they have been assigned. No more, no less.

#2: Once they have said a line, they cannot speak again until after another player has said a line of their own. This is because until another player speaks, any new words would still technically be part of the same line and take the word limit over their allowance per line.

#3: To ensure the lines are being kept to the correct length try not to talk over another player or interject in their sentences. Doing so will muddy the waters and make it unclear if the game is being played correctly.

How does the game end? This game is ended by the Emcee when they feel it's reached a good point to end it, or the players can end it if they find a natural conclusion.

Pro Tip #1: You can have fun with your limited number of words. If you can say only one or two words you can lean on physicality to express yourself.

You can also make a limited number of words seem more meaningful if you say them with a 'wise knowing' look on your face, and a confidence in your delivery of the line.

Pro Tip #2: If you need to use your fingers to count the number of words you've said in a line...do it! If this is the case, I'd also say don't hide it. The audience will enjoy the fact that you need fingers to help you count to five.

3: INCREASE

Emcee Intro Script: In this game, every time an actor speaks, the lines they say will have an increasing number of words.

So, when the performers say their first lines, they will say one word each. And then their next lines will have two words each. Their third lines will be three words each, and this increase will continue to four, five and so on.

Challenge Style: Scene based

Players: 2

Ask the audience for: A scenario such as a something you're searching for.

How to play the game:

#1: When each player says their first line, the line has to be one word long. This is followed by their second lines being two words long, their third being three words long and so on and so forth. This continues on in this fashion for the entirety of the scene until each player is effectively delivering monologues back and forth.

How does the game end? It will eventually become difficult for both the audience and the players to be able to keep track of how many words each player is saying. At this point it would be a good idea to end the scene.

Pro Tip #1: If you need to use your fingers to count out words...do it.

Pro Tip #2: The flow of this game gives a great opportunity to explore why the characters have so little to say to each other at the start and why it develops so they will say long speeches to each other by the end. Are they shy and become more comfortable? Is it a debate or argument that builds over time? The choice is yours!

4: QUESTION KOMBAT

Emcee Intro Script: Our next challenge is called Question Kombat. In Question Kombat two players will perform a scene in which everything they say has to be a question. They are not allowed to say any sentences that can be deemed a statement. They are also not allowed to leave extended pauses between questions or have a circular conversation.

If any of these rules are broken, the player will lose a life. They each start with five lives and the way we demonstrate losing lives is by losing a limb.

If they lose one life, they must continue the scene hopping. If they lose a second life, they will tuck an arm behind their back. A third is another arm, and the fourth is their other leg so they will continue the scene on their knees. If they lose a fifth life, then they lose their head and its game over.

Challenge Style: Scene based/Language challenge

Players: 2

Ask the audience for: A scenario such as a natural disaster.

How to play the game:

#1: Players can only speak in questions. They cannot say any sentences that would be considered statements. If you break this rule you lose a life.

For example you can say 'What's your name?' as it is a question.

But you are not allowed to say something like 'My name is Janet.' as this sentence is not a question.

You are also not allowed to say something like 'My name is Janet. What's yours?' as this is an example of a statement with a question attached. STRICTLY no statements are allowed.

#2: Tag on questions are not allowed either! This means sentences which whilst technically questions, are for the most part nonquestions with a tag on enquiry at the end turning them into questions.

For example, the sentence 'This is by far the worst town we have ever been to, isn't it?' is technically a question. However, for the understanding of the

Emcee and audience, this sounds exactly like a statement until the final two words.

Questions like this are problematic for two reasons. One, because they are too easy to create, and can be tagged onto practically every statement rendering the game too easy. And two, because a sentence like this will confuse both the Emcee who has to officiate the game, and the audience who are trying to keep track of it/enjoy it.

#3: Each player has five lives. When a player loses a life, they lose a limb! For example:

- First Life Lost: The player must continue the scene hopping on one leg.
- Second Life Lost: When the player loses a second life, they then tuck an arm behind their backs.
- Third Life Lost: A third life loss means that both arms will be tucked behind their backs.
- Forth Life Lost: Upon losing their fourth life, the player must go on both knees with both hands still behind their back.
- Fifth Life Lost: When a player loses their fifth life it is game over with the player symbolically losing their head!

#4: Hesitation Rule: If a player hesitates for an extended period of time without speaking, they lose a life.

#5: Circular Conversation Rule: A player will lose a life if they use the same questions over and over again. This can extend to repeated use of the same question types. For example, starting every question with 'Don't you think....'

How does the game end?

Question Kombat ends when one player has lost all their lives.

Pro Tip #1: Don't stand on the spot! As with almost any scene, you should try to keep the scene moving. If you lose a life and are stood on one leg, the visual of you hopping to move around the space is funny. Both players can have fun with saying things to get the other to hop around the stage.

Pro Tip #2: A single word can be a question. If one character believes they have recognised another they can simply say 'Rachel?' or 'Bob? etc to ask for confirmation, and through the inflection of your voice that becomes an question.

Lose a life...lose a limb...

5: QUESTIONS ONLY

Emcee Intro Script: The next game is called Questions Only. In this game, the performers will create a scene, but everything they say within the scene has to be a question. If they say anything that isn't a question, or hesitate for too long, they will be replaced in the scene by another performer.

Challenge Style: Scene based/Language challenge

Players: 2+

Ask the audience for: A starting point, such as a well-known TV show.

Setup: Any players not actively in the scene stand in the wings or on a back line waiting to enter the scene whilst the players actively in the scene use the playing space on the stage. If a player is eliminated, they leave the playing space and go back to the wings/back line.

How to play the game:

 # 1: Everything you say must be a question. You're not allowed to say any sentences that would be deemed as statements.

#2: Hesitation. If you hesitate for too long, you will be eliminated and replaced in the scene by another performer (if more than two players are playing)

#3: Circular conversation rule. Don't get stuck in a loop asking the same questions repeatedly, or asking the same question back that was just asked to you, or by starting all of your questions in the same way.

#4: When a player goes wrong, they are replaced in the scene by another player. The new player joining the scene will be a brand new character and not a continuation of the eliminated player's character.

How does the game end?

The game ends when the Emcee feels enough time has passed or the scene has run its course.

Pro Tips #1: Try to vary up your questions. If you start different sentences with who, what, when, why, where, or how, they will usually end up as a question. Try to use all of these throughout the scene.

Pro Tip #2: Try to avoid starting every sentence with 'Don't you think...' or 'Did you know...' as it can be easy to get into a pattern where you say these phrases followed by any fact and it will be a question. This will remove the sense of challenge from the game and you'll turn off your audience.

Pro Tip #3: If you are joining a scene which is already in progress make sure you join the scene as if you have just arrived. Whilst 'you the actor' will have seen the scene up to this point, it's not always likely that your character will have seen and heard everything that has just happened.

6: STATEMENTS ONLY

Emcee Intro Script: The next game is Statements Only. In this game, the performers will create a scene, but everything they say within it has to be a statement. If they say anything that is a question, and isn't a statement, or if they hesitate for too long, they will be replaced in the scene by another performer.

Challenge Style: Scene based/Language challenge.

Players: 2+

1 vs 1 (with each player having 5 lives)

Teams of up to 5 vs 5 (each player has 1 life)

Note: There are only two active players at any one time. Teams of up 5 vs 5 can compete in an elimination style, but there will only be two players competing actively in the scene.

Ask the audience for: A scenario such as something you may need to confess to another person.

Setup: Any players not actively in the scene stand in the wings or on a back line waiting to enter the scene whilst the players actively in the scene use the playing space on the stage. If a player is eliminated, they leave the playing space and return to the wings/back line.

How to play the game:

#1: Everything the performers say must be a statement. They are not allowed to say sentences that can be interpreted as questions.

#2: No hesitation! This game can become extremely easy if a player has enough thinking time. Make sure you keep the pace up of your delivery up, and also in making sure there are no gaps big between players lines.

#3: Circular conversation rule. Make sure you don't use a limited vocabulary of words. "Look the chair! There is the chair. I found the chair. The chair is there!" is an example of sentences that don't break the rules, but also don't advance the scene. Keep your language varied.

How does the game end?

Either when all players have been eliminated, or when the Emcee feels the scene has run its course.

Pro Tip #1: Don't play it safe! If you use a slow delivery in the way you speak, or a limited vocabulary this game will become too easy to 'win'. And the effect of this will make it look like you're trying too hard to win, and then the audience may want you to lose.

Don't be afraid of making mistakes as the audience will gravitate to you more if you are more daring and are willing to make mistakes rather than play it safe.

7: QUESTIONS AND STATEMENTS

Emcee Intro Script: The following game is Questions and Statements. In this game, the performers will create a scene, and at regular intervals the Emcee will call out either 'Questions Only' or 'Statements Only' and from that points on, the performers will only be allowed to speak in either questions or statements.

Challenge Style: Scene based/Language challenge

Players: 2+

Ask the audience for: A scenario such as where you'd go on a day out.

Setup: Any players not actively in the scene stand in the wings or on a back line waiting to enter the scene when it is their turn. If a player is eliminated, they leave the playing space and go to the wings/back line.

How to play the game:

#1: When playing in Questions Only mode, you can only speak in questions. Nothing you say is allowed to be deemed a statement. If you do say a statement, you will be eliminated.

#2: When you are playing in Statements Only mode, you must only speak in statements. You are not allowed to ask any questions. If you do ask a question, you will be eliminated.

#3: Avoid hesitations in the dialogue. If you do hesitate, you will be eliminated.

#4: Avoid circular conversations that go nowhere. If you do, you will at first receive a 'circular conversation warning' and if you continue, you will be eliminated.

How does the game end?

It ends when either all players have been eliminated or when the Emcee decides the scene has run its course.

Pro Tip #1: Keep your conversation pace up. This game can become very easy if you have a very slow delivery, or if you leave big pauses in between lines.

Don't give yourself loads of thinking time. It's generally more entertaining if you're more daring and have the mind set of 'just keep going without thinking about it too much.'

Pro Tip #2: Keep the story going forwards. It's easy to get stuck in your own head when switching back and forth between questions only and statements only as your brain power is being used on the rules of the game. Don't worry so much about making mistakes in the rules of the game, and instead focus on driving the story forwards.

Pro Tip #3: Answer your own questions! If you are currently speaking in questions only, and the Emcee calls out 'Statements Only' it gives you the opportunity to answer whatever your last question was yourself. For Example:

Player 1: Who ate all the cake?

Emcee: Statements only!

Player 1: I know it was you!

Of course player 2 could also have used this opportunity to answer in the same way, but there is something satisfying about the scenario where you get to have both the questioning line and the statement reply.

The reverse also works where you can be speaking in statements only and can then ask a follow up question when the game switches to questions only. For example:

Player 1: This is the best cake in the world.

Emcee: Questions only!

Player 1: ...isn't it?

I'm improvising Jack!

8: KEYBOARD WARRIORS

Emcee Intro Script: This next game is called Keyboard Warriors and is one of the most challenging games out there. With smart phones and social media, we've become used to shortening our spelling and speech further and further so that sometimes we end up just speaking in letters rather than actual words. L O L. And in this game our players are only allowed to communicate by saying the names of keys you would find on a computer keyboard.

Challenge Style: Scene Based/Language challenge

Players: 2-4

Ask the audience for: A scenario such as a crisis at work.

How to play the game:

#1: The players are only allowed to say the names of keys you would find on a typical QWERTY keyboard in order to communicate. This means letters can only be pronounced as the names of each letter and not as other sounds which that letter can be used in general speech to make.

For example, the letter 'W' could only be pronounced as 'Double You' and not as the sound as heard at the beginning of words such as water, wish or words.

This restriction will massively limit your vocabulary, but it is possible to say two or more letters one after another to give the illusion of saying normal words. Such as:

- P.N.O – piano
- L.O – hello
- P.T – the name Petey
- S.A – essay

#2: In addition to being able to say the name of letters, you can also say the numbers that appear on the keyboard which can be used in a variety of ways to make additional words as well as being used as the numbers themselves. For example:

- U.F.1.A.TV! – You have won a TV.
- I.M.6.E – I am sexy

#3: Lastly as well as letters and numbers a keyboard also features several other keys which give select words that can be used outright, or in combination with the letters or numbers to create new words. For example:

- A.U! Shift.Down.2.Escape.@.D.End – Hey you! Shift down to escape at the end.

How does the game end? This is a particularly difficult game to play, so don't expect it to last very long. The Emcee should call time on the scene as soon as they see that the players are running out of steam, and before they get completely stuck.

Pro Tip #1: Don't rush your words. You'll want the audience to be able to clearly hear all the letters you are saying as individual sounds, so don't say things too fast.

For example if you said 'L.O. R.U.O.K?' it should still be recognisable that you are saying the names of the letters and not just saying the words 'Hello. Are you OK?'

Your task is to say the names of individual keys, so embrace the slight staccato delivery to highlight to the audience when you are achieving the rules of the game.

Additionally, as this is a very challenging game, if you rattle through your material too fast the scene will be over in a blink of an eye.

Pro Tip #2: Use repetition. Don't be afraid to repeat words or sentences two or three times in this game. This will give the audience more opportunity to understand the sentences you are saying, and more thinking time for you and your scene partners to form their next sentences. You can also use the repetition to heighten an emotion or show an attitude towards another character.

Pro Tip #3: Use fun character voices to emphasise the sometimes-strange pronunciations of words this game forces on you. The word piano sounds slightly unusual when pronounced as P.N.O, but it is close enough that your audience should understand it. Other words may not be quite as clear, but you may be able to make them sound more acceptable to the ear if you play around with character voices and accents.

9: ACRONYMS

Emcee Intro Script: Now we're going to play A Captivating Rambunctious Oral Noir You Might Say...or Acronyms for short. Yes, this game will see our improvisers create acronyms based on words or descriptions of your choosing.

Challenge Style: Language challenge

Players: 1+

Ask the audience for:

#1: Interesting words that can be used as the acronyms.

Or #2: Descriptions of businesses.

How to play the game:

Note: This game can be played in two ways. Either:

#1: The player is given a word suggested by the audience. They then have to turn that word into an acronym by saying what each letter of the word stands for. After this, they must describe where this acronym would be found.

For example: If the word was 'FIRE' a player could say that 'FIRE' stands for the 'Flatulence Institution's Royal Ensemble' or FIRE for short, and then proceed to give a brief description of what that organisation does.

#2: The second way the game is played is by asking the audience for a type of business and then creating a suitable name and acronym for it.

For example: If the audience has requested you create an acronym for a milk company you could say that it made you think of the Universal Dairy Drink Extreme Revolution Society, or UDDERS for short. And then give further info on how this milk company operates.

#3: The Emcee can either set this challenge as a task to individual players, or they can set the challenge to all players who can choose to step forward to answer in a quick fire style.

How does the game end? The Emcee will decide when enough acronyms have been described and end the game.

Pro Tip #1: If you need to give yourself a moment more thinking time to form your acronym you could always start with the description of the company and work towards explaining the acronym last.

SECTION 2: ALPHABETTI SPAGHETTI

Ah, the Alphabet Scene! A staple of any short form improv show. Now, before you say it, yes, an Alphabet Scene is still a language based game, but there's a good reason why the classic game gets a whole section dedicated to it in this book. Extreme Improv have continually created new takes on the simple concept to create a baker's dozen of games, each with their own tactics and challenges.

Some of these get ridiculously hard to play, but once mastered, you will have achieved legendary status as an alphabet wizard!

10: ALPHABET SCENE

Emcee Intro Script: The next challenge is a traditional Alphabet Scene. In an Alphabet Scene two performers will perform a scene in which every time a performer begins a new line of dialogue, they must begin the first word of the line with the next letter of the alphabet.

So for example if Player 1's first line started with a word that begins with the letter 'A', Player 2 must begin the next line of dialogue with a word that starts with the letter 'B'.

They will have 90 seconds to try to get all the way through the alphabet and end on the same letter they started on.

Challenge Style: Scene based/Language challenge.

Players: 2

Ask the audience for:

#1: A scenario – a place you may go for food.

#2: A letter of the alphabet for which the game will begin on.

Please note that the below examples all show the scenes starting on the letter A, but you can begin anywhere in the alphabet.

Set up: The Emcee should have a timer or stopwatch.

How to play the game:

#1: Every time a character starts speaking a new line of dialogue, the first word of the sentence must begin with the next letter of the alphabet following the pattern of A, B, C, D, E, F...etc.

#2: Players have 90 seconds to get all the way through the alphabet until 27 lines of dialogue have been spoken. The final line of dialogue will begin with the same letter of the alphabet that the scene began on.

For example:

Bob: **A**re you ok?

(Note that Bob's opening sentence begins with the letter A)

Jimmy: **B**ob I'm not feeling too well.

(And here Jimmy follows Bob's letter A by starting his sentence with a word that begins with a B)

Bob: **C**an I get you anything?

(Bob's reply continues this pattern by starting his next sentence with a word that begins with a C)

Jimmy: **D**rink of water please.

(As we can now see the scene is smoothly following the alphabet pattern of A, B, C, D, E, F etc...)

Bob: **E**vian water? Will that do?

How does the game end?

The scene will end once the performers have gone all the way through the alphabet and ended back on the same letter they began on, or when the 90 second time limit runs out.

Pro Tip #1: The trickiest letters are Q, K, Z and X. You can prepare for this game by thinking of some words that begin with each of these more challenging letters.

Pro Tip #2: Impress your audience by starting your sentences with words that relate to the scenario. For example, look at this scene set at an airport:

Bob: **A**irports are so frustrating. I hate waiting for my bags.

Jimmy: **B**aggage always lose my luggage.

Bob: **C**aptain, shouldn't we get on the plane soon?

Jimmy: **D**elta Airlines fired me this morning...

Pro Tip #3: Cheat to win. This is a game where you can occasionally break the rules to great comic effect. If you get to the letter 'X' you can sometimes say words such as 'eXactly' or 'eXpert' to cheat as you are actually saying words that begin with an E that sound like they begin with an X.

Likewise you could say the sentence 'YOU don't know me' to begin with the 'U', or 'WHY are you so annoying?' to begin with the letter 'Y'. Clearly these words don't begin with the correct letters, but you will get a bonus laugh out of the audience for your creativity. Be warned though that if you do it too much the audience will either groan or turn on you and potentially boo your cheating behaviour.

11: REVERSE ALPHABET SCENE

Emcee Intro Script: In a Reverse Alphabet Scene, two players will perform a scene where every time one of the performers speaks a new line of dialogue, the first word of that line must begin with the previous letter of the alphabet compared to what the actor who spoke before began their line with.

So, for purposes of this game we will be following the order of the alphabet that goes C, B, A rather than A, B, C.

They will go backwards through the alphabet until they have gone all the way through the alphabet and end on the same letter, they started the scene on. As with a traditional Alphabet scene, the performers will have 90 seconds to attempt to get through the entire alphabet!

Challenge Style: Scene based/Language challenge

Players: 2

Ask the audience for:

#1: A scenario – For example something you did on the weekend.

#2: A letter of the alphabet for which the game will begin on.

Setup: The Emcee should have a timer.

How to play the game:

#1: Every time a character starts speaking a new line of dialogue, the first word of the sentence must begin with the previous letter of the alphabet following the pattern of C, B, A, Z, Y, X, W...etc.

#2: Players have 90 seconds to get all the way through the alphabet until 27 lines of dialogue have been spoken. The final line of dialogue begins with the same letter of the alphabet that the scene began on.

For example:

Player 1: **Z**ara, your dinner is ready.

(Note that Player 1's opening sentence begins with the letter Z)

Player 2: **Y**uk! Who made this?

(And here Player 2 follows up by starting the next line with the previous letter: Y)

Player 1: **X**ander made it just for you.

(Player 1's reply continues this pattern by starting the next sentence with a word that begins with a X)

Player 2: **W**hat on earth is in this stew?

(and so on...)

Player 1: **V**ery good question. I think it's meant to be beef.

How does the game end?

The scene will end once the performers have gone all the way through the alphabet and ended back on the same letter they began on, or when the 90 second time limit has been reached.

Pro Tip #1: It can be difficult to play a normal Alphabet Scene, so don't be afraid to call upon the audience to help you out if you're stuck on which letter is next if you get lost. They'll enjoy this and it will help keep things going.

Pro Tip #2: You only have 90 seconds to complete this game, so don't make the first five lines a monologue each. Mix in longer and shorter lines, and as the timer is running out you can give a greater sense of urgency to speed up the conversation.

12: QWERTY ALPHABET SCENE

Emcee Intro Script: In a QWERTY Alphabet Scene, two players will start each line of dialogue with the next letter of the alphabet, following the order of keys as found on a QWERTY keyboard. This is the keyboard you'd find on a computer or on your smart phone.

So, for example Player 1 will start a sentence where the first word begins with the letter 'Q' and then Player Two will follow this with a sentence that begins with the letter 'W'. Followed by E, then R, T, Y and so on.

Expect the performers to get stuck, so if you have your phone to hand, be a good Samaritan and shout the correct letter at them when they go wrong!

Finally, the performers will have 90 seconds to complete the scene!

Challenge Style: Scene based/Language challenge.

Players: 2

Ask the audience for: A scenario such as returning an unwanted gift to a shop.

How to play the game:

#1: You can see the basic rules for an alphabet scene in the section for the standard or Reverse Alphabet games. However, the big change here is the alphabet no longer follows the order of A, B, C etc. In this game the alphabet follows the order of the keys laid out on any QWERTY keyboard.

Q-W-E-R-T-Y-U-I-O-P-A-S-D-F-G-H-J-K-L-Z-X-C-V-B-N-M

Example:

Player 1: **Q**uiet! Do you hear a noise?

(Note that Player 1's opening sentence begins with the letter Q)

Player 2: **W**hat kind of noise was it?

(And here Player 2 follows Player 1's letter Q by starting their sentence with a W as that is next on a QWERTY keyboard)

Player 1: **E**vil whispers are coming from behind the walls!

Player 2: **R**un away before the demons find us!

Player 1: **T**ell you what. How about I run and you fight the demon?!

Player 2: **Y**ou're kidding right?

Player 1: **I**'m not kidding at all...

As you can see from the above example the basic rules of any alphabet scene still apply. It is just the order of the letters that have been altered.

How does the game end?

The scene will end once the performers have gone all the way through the QWERTY alphabet and ended on the final letter which is M.

Pro Tips #1: Learn the QWERTY alphabet and not only will you boss the game, but you'll be able to impress your friends at parties! You can make the QWERTY alphabet fit to the same basic tune as the traditional alphabet song by following this pattern:

QWE-RTY-UIO-PAS-DFGHJKL-ZXC-VBNM. Now I know my QWE I don't need to know my ABC.

Pro Tip #2: Don't be afraid to look to your audience for help when you're stuck on a letter. They'll be on your side to get it right and will feel more involved to help you.

13: THE REVERSE QWERTY ALPHABET SCENE

Description of the Game: This is a game you are unlikely to play, and you can probably work out the rules if you've read the last few variations of an Alphabet Scene.

I've included brief descriptions of all of the reverse versions of all the Alphabet Scenes in the book for the purpose of warning you of the pitfalls of playing them.

This game follows the same rules as a regular QWERTY Alphabet scene, but the order of the letters goes backwards. So, the order would now be:

M-N-B-V-C-X-Z-L-K-J-H-G-F-D-S-A-P-O-I-U-Y-T-R-E-W-Q

Learned it yet? Doesn't matter if you have as the audience will probably be too confused as to what you're attempting...except that one guy with his phone out checking every sentence you say rather than watching the scene!

14: DVORAK ALPHABET SCENE

Emcee Intro Script: An almost impossible challenge, the Dvorak Alphabet Scene is played by two players who must perform a scene where every time the next player starts a line of dialogue, the sentence must begin with a word that begins with the next letter in the Dvorak Alphabet Keyboard layout.

The order of the alphabet will not follow the traditional ABC pattern, or even the QWERTY pattern as seen on most computer or smart device keyboards. Instead the players must follow the rarely seen alphabet order that is found on the widely rejected Dvorak keyboard as devised by August Dvorak in 1936.

Challenge Style: Scene based/Language challenge

Players: 2

Ask the audience for: Mercy on your souls for attempting this...plus a place of work.

How to play the game:

#1: You can see the basic rules for an alphabet scene in the section for the standard, Reverse or QWERTY Alphabet games. However, the big change here is the alphabet no longer follows the order of A, B, C etc. In this game the alphabet follows the order of the keys laid out on any Dvorak keyboard which goes:

P-Y-F-G-C-R-L-A-O-E-U-I-D-H-T-N-S-Q-J-K-X-B-M-W-V-Z

How does the game end?

The scene will end once the performers have gone all the way through the Dvorak alphabet and ended on the letter Z.

What the hell is the Dvorak Keyboard?

It is a keyboard layout from 1936. Devised by a chap called August Dvorak, and his brother in law William Dealey (thanks Wikipedia). It was designed as an alternative keyboard layout to the QWERTY one we use today. It is supposedly a more efficient layout that can allow for quicker typing and less errors. It didn't catch on, but it's still known enough for us to justify that an Extreme Improv game can be made in its honour. Dvorak...we salute you!

Example Scene:

Player 1: **P**eter can we go shopping please?

Player 2: **Y**ou forgot to buy Bill a present, didn't you?

Player 1: **F**ine make me feel bad about it.

Player 2: **G**ot any idea what you will buy him?

Player 1: **C**ould buy him a Dvorak keyboard...

Player 2: **R**eally? What on earth is that???

You get the idea! As with the QWERTY alphabet game you'll be following a letter order that the audience won't know. And unlike the QWERTY game where they could check it on their phones or maybe have a cat in hell's chance of knowing what comes next... here they will not!

Pro Tip #1: Learn the Dvorak alphabet and not only will you confuse your friends at parties, but you'll have also wasted several hours of your life learning something that really has no purpose outside this game!

You can make the Dvorak alphabet fit to the same basic tune as the traditional alphabet song by following this:

PYFG-CRL-AOEU-IDH-TNSQJKX-BMW-V and Z. Now I know my PYFG I don't need to know my ABC.

Pro Tip #2: Don't be afraid to look to your audience for help when you're stuck on a letter. They won't be able to help you, but they'll be on your side and enjoy watching you struggle!

15: THE REVERSE DVORAK ALPHABET SCENE

Description of the Game: OK, this is getting ridiculous now. So I've included this game in the list in the interest of being complete, but will only include this brief description to tell you why you shouldn't play it in your show.

As you can imagine from the title, the game is the same as the regular Dvorak Alphabet game, but the order of the letters is in reverse. Unless you are performing this to language scholars at Oxford University the chances are that no one watching will even know the Dvorak alphabet going forwards, let alone backwards. Don't do it!

16: NATO PHONETIC ALPHABET SCENE

Emcee Intro Script: The next challenge is what we call the NATO Phonetic Alphabet Scene. In this challenge, two players will perform a scene in which every time a performer starts a line of dialogue, the line must begin with the subsequent letter of the NATO Phonetic Alphabet.

But unlike a normal alphabet game where they will say a word beginning with each letter, here they must begin each line with the name of each letter. Alpha, Bravo, Charlie etc... until they have reached Zulu.

Challenge Style: Scene based/Language challenge

Players: 2

Ask the audience for: A scenario such as an activity you do on rainy days.

How to play the game:

 # 1: In a NATO Phonetic Alphabet game, the players must start each line of dialogue by saying the name of the next letter of the NATO Phonetic Alphabet.

For example:

Player 1: **Alpha** male in the house!

Player 2: **Bravo!** You destroyed your opponent at boxing!

Player 1: **Charlie** my friend, I could not have done it without you.

Player 2: **Dealt a** harsh loss to the former champion.

Player 1: **Echo**s of the punch could be heard for miles.

And so on...

Pro Tip #1: At first it may seem as if there is only one way to use each word from the NATO Phonetic Alphabet, but with practice and experimentation you will find there are multiple ways to use many of the words to create lots of possibilities for how the scene can progress. For example, let's look at the some of the ways the words can be interpreted differently:

Alpha: 'Alpha males are so annoying.' Or 'Al for goodness sake.' Or 'Alf or Bill stole my cheese.'

India: 'India is where I bought these shoes.' Or 'In dear? Dear are you in yet?' Or 'Ind-here' - pronounced with emphasis to mean 'in here'

Full NATO Phonetic Alphabet

Here is the full NATO Phonetic Alphabet. Feel free to write your ideas next to each word for how it can be used and/or manipulated to work as part of the game.

- Alpha
- Bravo
- Charlie
- Delta
- Echo
- Foxtrot
- Golf
- Hotel
- India
- Juliet
- Kilo
- Lima
- Mike
- November
- Oscar
- Papa
- Quebec
- Romeo
- Sierra
- Tango
- Uniform
- Victor
- Whisky
- X-ray
- Yankee
- Zulu

17: THE REVERSE NATO PHONETIC ALPHABET SCENE

Description of the Game: Yup, you can probably guess how this works. The Reverse NATO Phonetic Alphabet Game works exactly like the normal NATO Phonetic Alphabet Game, but the order of the letters goes backwards.

The audience have a reasonable chance of being able to follow this game, as the NATO Phonetic Alphabet is common enough so they will know if you've got the right words in the correct reverse order. However it's not a highly recommended game to play as it would be best played after the audience have seen a normal NATO Phonetic Alphabet scene, and by that point you're likely to have used several of the letters to their best effect already.

18: GREEK ALPHABET SCENE

Emcee Intro Script: In a Greek Alphabet scene, two players will perform a scene in which every time a player begins their next line of dialogue, the line must begin with them saying the next letter of the Greek Alphabet.

For clarity we don't mean words that begin with the next letter, we mean the name of the next letter itself – Alpha, Beta, Gamma etc

Challenge Style: Scene based/Language challenge

Players: 2

Ask the audience for: A scenario such as a crime you would like to commit.

How to play the game:

#1: Unlike normal Alphabet Scenes, which sees two players start each line of dialogue with the next letter of the alphabet, the Greek Alphabet game sees the players start each line with the name of the letter. They will use the name of each letter as if it were the first word.

For example:

Player 1: **Al for** once will you shut up. (Alpha)

Player 2: **Bate her** much more and your wife will kill you. (Beta)

Player 1: **Gamma** radiation must have affected her like the Hulk. (Gamma)

Player 2: **Dealt her** a rough fate marrying you. (Delta)

Player 1: **Epsilon** was the name of her lover... (Epsilon)

Pro Tip 1: Unlike the NATO Phonetic Alphabet game, the Greek alphabet has many more unusual and uncommon sounding words such as epsilon, omicron, sigma and upsilon. To tackle such words that cannot easily be repurposed into English words you have to get creative.

Names: Epsilon sounds like it may be an uncommon surname or name of a medicine. Don't struggle and just embrace it as a made-up word which your audience will be able to understand from the context of the rest of your sentence.

Here's a few ideas on how some of the unusual words can be used:

Sigma:

- Cig ma? – as in a request for a cigarette from your mother.
- Sigma Freud – as a close version of the name Sigmund Freud

Upsilon:

- Sup Si lon...g time no see! – as in 'What's up Simon? Long time no see.

The Full Greek Alphabet

Here is the full Greek Alphabet. Feel free to write your ideas next to each word for how it can be used and/or manipulated to work as part of the game.

- Alpha
- Beta
- Gamma
- Delta
- Epsilon
- Zeta
- Eta
- Theta
- Iota
- Kappa
- Lambda
- Mu
- Nu
- Xi
- Omicron
- Pi
- Rho
- Sigma
- Tau
- Upsilon
- Phi
- Chi
- Psi
- Omega

19: THE REVERSE GREEK ALPHABET SCENE

Description of the Game: You get the idea by now. The Reverse Greek Alphabet Game works exactly like the Greek Alphabet Game, but the order of the letters goes backwards.

This is a rarely played game as the audience are unlikely to know the Greek alphabet well enough going forwards to appreciate it going backwards. If you can do it, great, but the main effect the game will have is that it sounds impressively challenging when you announce the rules before you actually play it!

If you do play this game, do it with confidence, and only challenge players who have practised it in rehearsals to perform it in a show, or the game is likely to fall flat!

20: RANDOM ALPHABET GAME

Emcee Intro Script: The ultimate mind melter, the Random Alphabet Game is part improv scene, part game of bingo, and part game of Russian Roulette!

The performers will create a scene in which every time a player starts a new line of dialogue it must begin with a letter of the alphabet that hasn't been used to start a line of dialogue in the scene already.

And what's more, the players have to use the letters in a random order.

I will keep score of what letters have already been used to start a line to make sure the players don't repeat a letter. And I will also make sure the players are not using letters in any recognisable pattern. Patterns such as ABCD, DCBA, and QWERTY will result in a disqualification.

The players will have 2 minutes to complete the scene and use all the letters! If the time runs out, the player whose turn it is loses! If the players successfully use all the letters, they both win! If one player repeats a letter or uses a pattern that player loses, and the other player wins.

Challenge Style: Scene based/Language challenge

Players: 2

Ask the audience for: A scenario such as training for a sport.

Setup: A stopwatch would be useful to keep time.

How to play the game:

#1: The two players have 2 minutes to perform a scene where every time the next player starts a sentence, the line of dialogue must begin with a letter that hasn't been used to start a line before.

#2: Once a letter has been used as a beginning letter it cannot be used again to start a new sentence. To do so will mean the offending player loses the game.

#3: If the scene is not completed within 2 minutes whoever's turn it is to speak loses the game and the other player wins.

#4: Anti pattern rule: In a Random Alphabet Game you are not allowed to follow an established pattern of the alphabet either individually or as a team. For example if Player 1 starts a line with the word 'Banana' Player 2 could not then start a line with words beginning with A or C as they are next to the letter B.

#5: The Emcee will have to keep check of what letters have been used already. I'd suggest writing down the whole alphabet and checking them off when they're used, like in a game of Bingo.

Pro Tip #1: As this is a competitive game you can have fun with trying to trip the other player up. If you feel they're struggling to remember which letters have already been used to start lines you could vary the length of your lines either to be longer or very short which would put the pressure back on them to think of another unused letter.

Pro Tip #2: Additionally you can purposely say words such as eye and I or you and ewe as a tactic to make the other player think you have used different letters then you actually have. The context of the sentence you say should reveal which spelling the word would have, but as a warning don't be surprised if you also create confusion for the Emcee and this could therefore work against you.

21: THE ANCIENT EGYPTIAN HIEROGLYPHICS SCENE

Emcee Intro Script: Our next challenge is a spin on a traditional Alphabet Scene. Instead of using the English, or more accurately the Latin alphabet, we will create a scene where the first word of each line of dialogue will be inspired by a picture of an ancient Egyptian hieroglyph. We will display a graph of some randomly selected hieroglyphics so that both the performers and the audience will see them at the same time.

Challenge Style: Scene Based

Players: 2

Ask the audience for:

A scenario – For example an unusual job.

Setup: For this game you will need a projector, a large printed chart or a chalk/white board where you can display a selection of 25-30 Egyptian hieroglyphs. These will need to be visible to both the performers and the audience to be able to follow the game.

How to play the game:

#1: Every time a character starts speaking a new line of dialogue, the first word of the sentence must be inspired by the picture that represents the hieroglyph.

For example:

If the chart of hieroglyphs shows a bird, a foot, a cup, a snake, water and a man, the dialogue could go as follows:

Player 1: Tweeted the government this morning. Not happy with the tax increases! (Bird)

Player 2: Kick up the pants. It's what they deserve! (Foot)

Player 1: Cheers! I'll drink to that! (Cup)

Player 2: Hiss! Boo! I'm gonna heckle them on the march tomorrow. (Snake)

Player 1: Water cannons is what the police are using to move on the protesters. (Water)

Player 2: Man that sucks. We need a new plan. (Man)

How does the game end?

The scene will end once the performers have gone all the way through the selection of hieroglyphs on display.

Pro Tip #1: The way you can interpret the hieroglyphs can be literal or non-literal. As an example a picture of a snake could lead you to start your sentence with the word 'snake' as the picture is literally a snake. Alternatively, it could be used to represent the word 'Hiss' as it is the sound a snake makes. Additionally you could look at the picture of a snake and interpret it as slither, reptile, slimy (even though snakes aren't slimy – it's a common misconception) fangs and so on. So you could look at a snake and your sentence be 'Fangs for giving me that' as in 'Thanks for giving me that.'

22: THE ROSETTA STONE

Emcee Intro Script: The next improv challenge is called Rosetta Stone. One of our performers will be presented with a transcript of a text written in ancient Egyptian hieroglyphs and be tasked with translating the symbols into English to tell the story that is written.

Challenge Style: Monologue

Players: 1

Ask the audience for:

Potentially nothing. You could let the performer work completely from the hieroglyphs, but if you want to involve audience interaction you can ask the audience for an event or place where the story is set.

Setup: For this game you will need a projector, a large printed chart or a chalk/white board where you can display a selection of 25-30 Egyptian hieroglyphs. These will need to be visible to both the performer and the audience to be able to follow the game.

How to play the game:

#1: The performer reads the hieroglyphs out loud, putting words in between each symbol to turn it into a story.

#2: The hieroglyph symbols should be the main focus of the story and other words used should just bridge gaps between them. You should try to have at least one symbol represented per sentence if not more.

How does the game end?

The game will end once the performers have gone all the way through the selection of hieroglyphs on display.

Pro Tip #1: If possible, try to combine multiple hieroglyph symbols to represent single words or ideas. For example, a building symbol followed by an insect could be combined to become a housefly. Or maybe a house followed by a fly represents a tornado.

SECTION 3: STYLE IT OUT

The games in this section all see regular changes in the scenes being performed. This can range from a change in story or a change in genre to a change in game style or emotion you have to use...or any other style in between!

In the game Jekyll and Hyde characters can swap between having good and evil personalities.

23: FREEZE TAG

Emcee Intro Script: We're now going to play the game Freeze Tag. The way it works is that two players will start creating a scene and at any time another performer can call out 'Freeze'.

When they have done this the performers in the scene freeze exactly as they are. Then the player who called freeze will tag one of the frozen players out of the scene. They will then assume the position the frozen player was stood in and create a brand new scene based on the pose.

Challenge Style: Scene based

Players: 3+

Ask the audience for: An initial physical pose for the first two players.

Setup: Two players take centre stage whilst all other players either wait at the side of the stage, in the wings or on a back line waiting to enter the scene at a good opportunity.

How to play the game:

#1: The first two players in the scene start performing a scene inspired by the physical pose that was suggested by the audience member.

#2: Another player not currently active in the scene calls out the word 'Freeze' when they see a physical pose within the scene that they believe they can take advantage of.

#3: The players in the scene freeze physically until the new player taps one of them on the shoulder to tag them out of the scene. The player who has been tagged out exits the scene.

#4: The new player assumes the same physical pose that the exiting player was stood in, and then creates a new scene based on this pose.

Note that the new player should create a brand new scene which is not a continuation of the scene that was already in progress. Even though one of the performers on stage was already on stage they also become a new character as well.

#5: It should be the responsibility of the new player entering the scene to deliver the first line of dialogue. This follows the logic that if a player has chosen this moment to freeze and interrupt a scene, it is because they have a new idea, and shouldn't leave the responsibility on the player already in the scene to create the new idea.

This approach also means you won't have any confusion over which player should deliver the first line of the new scene.

#6: This process can repeat over and over again with players calling freeze to enter and create new scenes.

How does the game end? The Emcee should end the game once they judge that a suitable number of new scenes have been created.

Pro Tip #1: Don't block ideas. If a player tags in and creates a new scene you should always take the attitude of saying 'yes and' to whatever their opening line is. This doesn't mean that you have to literally say the phrase 'yes and' (although never a bad thing) but rather that you accept the offer of a new idea being given to you.

Pro Tip #2: Make sure you give enough time for a new scene to be established before you call freeze on it. It's common, especially amongst younger players who are keen to have a turn to instantly call 'Freeze' as soon as a new scene has started so that they can take over and have a go. This is an easy mistake to make, so to avoid making it, make sure you give at least 20 or 30 seconds for the scene in progress to have time to develop.

Pro Tip #3: Don't let your fellow performers remain stuck in a scene for an eternity. If the performers in the scene have been in there for 1-2 minutes, it's probably more than enough time for their scene to have played out.

This point would be good for you to call 'Freeze' and take over and create a new scene. Even if you can't see an award-winning physical pose that will lead to an incredible idea, just take over and do something until inspiration hits.

Pro Tip #4: Use lots of physicality to give the players plenty of opportunities to call 'Freeze.' The players who aren't actively in the scene will be watching the performing players closely, as they are waiting for a physical pose to inspire a new scene.

If you are actively in the scene and just stand there it won't give any opportunities for the non-active players to call freeze. By having varied physicality such as using more than average amounts of arm and hand gestures, standing/sitting, hopping etc, it will give the non-active players lots of opportunities to spark inspiration from your poses.

24: FILM AND THEATRE STYLES

Emcee Intro Script: In a game of Film and Theatre styles, the performers will create a scene based on an audience suggestion. Every so often I will pause the action of the scene by calling 'freeze' and will take an audience suggestion of a film, television or theatre genre which the performers must continue the scene in the style of.

Challenge Style: Scene based/Styles challenge

Players: 2-4

Ask the audience for:

#1: Initial scene scenario idea. This could be a place of work, or some kind of relationship or dilemma.

#2: Additionally throughout the scene: Ask the audience for suggestions of Film, Television and Theatre genres for the players to continue the scene in the style of.

How to play the game:

#1: The game begins with the performers creating a scene without any particular style attached to it. It is just a 'normal' scene.

#2: Whenever the Emcee calls 'Freeze' the performers on stage all literally freeze their physical positions. These poses may be useful when the game unfreezes as I'll explain below.

#3: The Emcee will ask the audience for a suggestion of a film, television or theatre genre for the performers to continue the scene in. Once selected the Emcee will call Unfreeze, Continue, or Action for the scene to continue.

#4: The actors will now continue the same story from where it left off, but will layer it with references and conventions from the genre that audience suggested.

#5: The Emcee will call 'Freeze' again after a short while (usually 30 seconds to a minute) and ask the audience for a new genre to continue in. This new genre will replace the previous genre. This process happens repeatedly throughout the scene.

How does the game end?

The Emcee can call for the scene to end once they feel the story has run its course or that the performers have done a reasonable number of different styles.

Pro Tip #1: As mentioned earlier, the poses you freeze in may be useful for when you unfreeze and continue a scene. By holding your position, you may find you can reinterpret the pose into something relevant to the next scenario.

For example if you have frozen with your arms up because a bank robber is holding a gun on you, and the new genre to continue in is a musical, you could easily change the arms being held up into swaying as part of a dance. This would fit the genre and would seem appropriate and quick thinking.

Pro Tip #2: Make sure you continue the same story you were already playing once you have the new genre to continue in. If the style called out is Star Wars, don't just recreate your favourite scene from The Last Jedi. You are still the same character as before but are continuing it in the style of Star Wars. This means if you were Jack and Jill fetching water, you are still Jack and Jill fetching water, but maybe you can use force powers to make the water float to you, or use a lightsabre or two along the way.

Here is a list of some of the various styles you may get suggestions of. If you are not familiar with any, it'd be useful to look them up to get an idea of what may be expected from the genre.

List of Film styles:

Action, Horror, Science Fiction, Rom Com, Comedy, Western, Swashbuckling Adventure, Film Noir, Thriller, Drama, War Film, Documentary, Fantasy, Slasher, Period Drama, Gangster, Zombie, Anime, Court Room Drama, Parody, Slapstick, Nicely Watchable, Silent Movie, 3D Movie, Disney, Superhero.

List of Television Styles:

Soap Opera, News Programme, Sports Programme, Documentary, Police Procedural, Children's TV, Cooking show, Music Video, Charity Telethon, Reality TV, Medical, Eurovision, Party Political Broadcast.

List of Theatre Styles:

Comedy, Tragedy, Historical play, Greek Tragedy, Melodrama, Oscar Wilde, Commedia dell'arte, Shakespeare, Musical Theatre, Physical Theatre, Theatre in Education, Pantomime, Restoration Comedy, Variety Show, Vaudeville, Interpretive Dance, Opera, Ballet, School Play, Fringe Theatre, Noh Theatre, Clowning, Mime, Puppet Show, Improv, Long form improv, Invisible Theatre, Street Theatre, Circus, Magician, Stand Up, Punch and Judy.

25: EMOTION OPTION

Emcee Intro Script: Our next game is Emotion Option. Our performers will start a scene, and every so often I will call out freeze! At this point I will ask the audience for various suggestions of emotions which the performers will have to display whilst continuing the scene.

Challenge Style: Scene based/Styles challenge

Players: 2-4

Ask the audience for: A scenario such as a problem at work.

How to play the game:

#1: The game starts with the performers creating a scene without any particular emotion attached to it. It is just a scene.

#2: Whenever the Emcee calls 'Freeze' the performers on stage all freeze their physical positions.

#3: The Emcee will ask the audience for a suggestion of an emotion for all the performers to display whilst they continue the scene. Once selected the Emcee will call 'Unfreeze' to continue the scene.

#4: The actors will now continue the same story from where it left off, but with a heightened sense of the suggested emotion.

#5: The Emcee will call 'Freeze' again after a short while (usually 30 seconds to a minute) and ask the audience for a new emotion to continue the scene. This new emotion will replace the previously suggested emotion. This process happens repeatedly throughout the scene.

How does the scene end?

The Emcee can call for the scene to end once they feel the story has run its course or that the performers have done a reasonable number of different emotion options.

Pro Tip #1: Don't let loud emotions create a wall of noise on stage. If you've been given emotions such as anger or excited don't just scream and cry and stamp about for 30 seconds. If everyone on stage does that the audience won't be able to hear anyone and will soon grow tired of it. Angry could be internalised with moments of outbursts, and crying could be sobbing as well as wailing.

List of Emotions and Feelings:

Happy, Sad, Angry, Loved, Scared, Disgusted, Joyful, Relieved, Pride, Hangry, Stressed, Hungry, Worried, Lonely, Lost, Heartbroken, Anxious, Confused, Giddy, Annoyed, Zany, Desperate, Terrified, In love, Bitter, Jealous, Indignant, Insulted, Irritated, Naughty, Flustered, Mad, Contrary, Offended, Sick, Ill, Perplexed, Content, Excited, Compassion, Miserable, Dizzy, Ambivalence.

26: STYLES CLASH

Emcee Intro Script: A Styles Clash is performed by 2-4 players who will perform a scene based on an audience suggestion.

Then every so often I will freeze the scene and ask the audience for a suggestion of a new style that the performers must continue the scene in.

This can include styles such as different genres of film/television/theatre, different emotions, animals, accents, time periods, or any other style I feel like asking the audience for.

Challenge Style: Scene based/Styles challenge

Players: 2-4

Ask the audience for: A scenario such as an ambition you had as a child.

How to play the game:

#1: The players start creating a scene based on the audience suggestion.

#2: When the Emcee calls out 'Freeze' the performers on stage all freeze in their current positions.

#3: At this point the Emcee asks the audience for a new style for the performers to continue the scene in. This could be a new style from the following categories:

- Film Style
- Theatre Style
- Television Style
- Emotion
- Accent
- Age of the Characters
- Time Period
- Medical conditions (Be careful not to cause offence)
- Accent
- Professions
- Book Style

- Animal
- Type of Object

Once selected, the performers continue the scene in that new style.

#4: After 30 seconds to a minute the Emcee will freeze the game again and repeat the process several times.

How does the game end?

A Styles Clash ends at the Emcee's discretion, once they feel the scene has reached a natural conclusion or that it is time to move to something else in the show.

Pro Tip #1: As with the others styles based games in this book, it's useful to know a few things that may come up with each style type. Knowing a little about a lot will give you plenty of reference points to use in the scenes.

Pro Tip #2: Always always make sure you keep the story moving forward. Don't fall into the trap of focussing purely on the new style and forgetting what the original story was supposed to be.

Pro Tip #3: Make sure that any new style you are given to continue the scene in replaces the old one. So, for example if your current style is Shakespeare, and then you're told to do the scene as cats, don't be Shakespearean cats. It may be funny to some degree, but you should always concentrate on continuing the story rather than carrying through every new style.

The concept of continuing multiple styles will be the focus of another game I'll cover in the book soon.

Pro Tip #4: Whilst on the subject of cats, do make sure that if you are told to continue the scene in the style of an animal that they are talking animals. It's much more difficult to continue the story of the scene if you are all just snarling and growling on stage compared to talking.

So, if you're told to be cats think Simba from The Lion King rather than your neighbour's cat. If you're told you're a dog then think of Brian from Family Guy rather than Santa's Little Helper from The Simpsons. Talking dogs can still scratch their ears and chase postmen like non-talking dogs, but they can also communicate a lot more clearly for the audience to follow the story.

To further this idea, you can use animal characteristics in place of human equivalents. A human may bring home a takeaway pizza, but a cat character may bring home a takeaway dead bird. A human may shake a hand, whereas a dog may sniff a butt as a greeting.

27: IMPROV GAME STYLES

Note: This game is best reserved towards the end of a show as it will re-use the rules of many games you are likely to have already played throughout the show. This way the audience will better understand the many different games' rules they will be seeing in quick succession.

Emcee Intro Script: The improv game to end all improv games! In Improv Game Styles, the players in the game will perform a scene based on an audience suggestion, and every so often I will call out 'Freeze'.

At this point I will instruct the players to continue playing the scene using the rules of another improv game.

So for example the first time the scene is frozen, the players may be asked to continue the scene under the rules of Questions Only, so the scene will continue where they can only speak in questions.

Then the next time I freeze the game, the players may be asked to continue the scene in the style of a Single Syllable Showdown. From this point the players will no longer have to speak in questions, but instead have to speak only in words of one syllable. This will continue for several changes of improv game styles!

Challenge Style: Multi

Players: 2-4

Ask the audience for: A scenario such as a problem to solve in the world.

Setup: For this game it may be useful to have chairs, microphones etc on standby. Make a plan of which other games will be revisited in this game so you're not stuck by asking the players to do something they're not able to do because something is missing.

How to play the game:

#1: The players begin a scene and continue until the Emcee calls freeze.

#2: Every so often the Emcee will call 'Freeze' to pause the action and change the improv game being played to the rules of another improv game. For example, at every 1-minute interval the rules could change in the following example pattern:

Normal scene > Questions only > Alphabet scene > Film and theatre styles > Single syllable

It is important that a single story continues throughout the entire scene and that the players don't restart or disconnect the story as the rules change from one game to another.

This game may be best played towards the end of a show so that the audience have seen individual versions of each of the games played first. This will help them understand the rules as they will have already seen the games played fully within the show.

Pro Tip #1: Throw yourself into this game with everything you have. The rules are going to change frequently, so you'll only have a few seconds per game to have fun with it and show your metal. If you go wrong or break rules – who cares?!

28: THE STACK

Emcee Intro Script: In a game of The Stack, the performers will create a scene based on an audience suggestion. Then periodically I will freeze the scene and add additional improv game rules that the players must continue the scene with.

So for example if I freeze the game and instruct the players to continue the scene as if it's a Western, the players must continue the scene in that genre. Then after a minute I may freeze the game again and 'Stack on' the rules of a Single Syllable Showdown.

So the players would have to continue the scene as both a Western and only speak in words of one syllable. I may then freeze them again and say 'stack on the rules of Questions Only'. So, from this point the game would become a Single Syllable Questions Only Western. And so on and so on until I have stacked on more and more improv challenges!

Challenge Style: Multi

Players: 2-4

Ask the audience for: A scenario such as an unusual place for a car to break down.

Setup: As with the game Improv Game Styles detailed elsewhere in this book, this may be a good game to save towards the end of your show as many of the rules you'll be putting on the performers will have already happened in other games.

And likewise, you may want to make sure you have chairs and microphones at the ready in case you need them for any of the games you are stacking on top of this scene.

How to play the game:

#1: The players start a normal scene without any rules attached and perform until the Emcee calls 'Freeze'.

#2: The Emcee will then set an improv game's rules to be played as the performers continue the scene. The players continue the story with the new game's rules for the remainder of the scene.

#3: After another 1 minute the Emcee calls freeze again. The Emcee will then add an additional improv game to also be played at the same time as the originally added game.

#4: This pattern continues with more and more improv games being stacked on top of each other.

How does the game end?

This pattern of the Emcee 'Stacking' additional improv game rules onto the scene continues until the game becomes too challenging for the players to continue any further, or a suitable end point is reached.

Here is an example of how the progression of the games being stack up could look:

- A scene set in a haunted house.
- A scene set in a haunted house, spoken in questions only.
- A scene set in a haunted house, spoken in questions only, but only using words of one syllable.
- A scene set in a haunted house, spoken in questions only, but only using words of one syllable and performed as a western.
- And so on and so forth.

Pro Tip #1: The point of this game is that you're being asked to do something very challenging. Don't be afraid to show off that you're succeeding! The more games that are added, feel free to over emphasise things that show you are achieving at the game, or enjoy getting stuck if you're struggling. The audience will be on your side to succeed.

Pro Tip #2: The longer the game goes on feel free to slow things down. This may contradict several games where I've said keeping the pace up will help you, but as you'll be playing several different games at once you will want to slow things down a bit so that the audience has a chance to keep up with what you're doing. Allow them a chance to take in each new game as you start playing it.

29: JEKYLL AND HYDE

Emcee Intro Script: The next game we will be playing is called Jekyll and Hyde. Inspired by the works of Robert Louis Stevenson, the scene will see one character continually flip back and forth between two sides of their personality. One good and the other evil. Acting as the voice in their head I will call either 'Jekyll' or 'Hyde' to signify the change between good and evil, respectively.

Challenge Style: Scene based

Players: 2-3

Ask the audience for: A practical problem you would like to solve.

How to play the game:

#1: Player 1 plays the character with the Jekyll and Hyde personality, and will always start the scene in the good natured Dr Jekyll persona.

Note that the character doesn't have to literally be Dr Jekyll/Mr Hyde – these terms are just to indicate good/bad, and your character can be anything you want or that the scene calls for.

#2: The performers create the scene, and whenever the Emcee calls 'Hyde' Player 1 has to take on a more evil, villainous version of their character. Likewise, whenever the Emcee calls 'Jekyll' Player 1's character will revert back to the nice version of the character.

This may or may not be obvious to the other characters in the scene. The Emcee calling Jekyll/Hyde shouldn't be acknowledged by the other players and they would only become aware of any changes through Player 1's actions.

How does the scene end? The scene will be ended at the Emcee's discretion.

Pro Tip #1: There are lots of options for how you could play the manifestation of the Jekyll/Hyde character. The character could demonstrate physical/vocal changes, changes in attitude, could have memories of their behaviour as the other version of themselves or not. This is up to the individual to play with.

Pro Tip #2: You can also play with how much the other characters do/do not have an awareness of the dual personalities of Player 1. It may be that other characters continually believe Player 1 to be a good person, and everything they do that is evil is behind the other player's backs. Or it could be that the other players gradually become aware that Player 1 is evil and may not believe when the good version of the character is present.

SECTION 4: RECREATIONAL RECREATION

The games in this section are all about the challenge of recreating performances previously given. Remakes, reboots, reimaginings and rebirths. These are recreational recreations!

If you did a headstand in a game of Verbatim, the following player would have to attempt to recreate it...or not!

30: VERBATIM

Emcee Intro Script:

Note: The Emcee intros are split into sections that should be said before each player has their turn in the game. Please read through the rules for the entire game to understand how it works and how these intro scripts fit in.

Emcee Intro Script 1: The next challenge is called Verbatim. In Verbatim, one player will perform a 30 second dramatic monologue on a theme of the audience's choosing.

Emcee Intro Script 2: (To be read after the first monologue)

Ok, now Player 2 will have 30 seconds to recreate Player 1's original monologue as precisely as they can. Here they go...

Emcee Intro Script 3: (To be read after the second monologue)

Right then, now Player 3 will have 30 seconds to recreate Player 2's recreation of Player 1's original monologue. For clarity, they are not recreating Player 1. They are just recreating the performance given by Player 2. Here goes...

Emcee Intro Script 4: (To be read after the third monologue)

So now we're gonna take things full circle. As Player 1 will now have 30 seconds to recreate player 3's recreation of Player 2's recreation of Player 1's own original monologue. Once again for clarity, they are not recreating themselves or Player 2, they are just recreating Player 3.

Emcee Intro Script 5: (To be read after the fourth and final monologue)

Well done! So, audience it is now up to you to vote. Who do you feel did the best recreation of what came before? And please remember that Player 1's original monologue is not up for scrutiny here. You are just voting on who did the best recreation. Player 1, 2 or 3?

Challenge Style: Monologue

Players: 3

Ask the audience for: A theme for a dramatic monologue.

Setup: A stopwatch or egg timer would be handy.

How to play the game:

#1: The first player is given 30 seconds to create a dramatic monologue.

#2: Once the first player has finished their monologue, a second player is given 30 seconds to recreate the original player's performance as precisely as they can.

#3: After the second player has recreated the first player's monologue, a third player will be given 30 seconds to recreate the second player's recreation of the original player's performance. Note that they are not trying to recreate the first player's performance. Their aim is to recreate the second player who performed directly before them. They should not include elements from the original monologue if the second player did not include them.

#4: After the third player has done their recreation, the Emcee will invite Player 1 to recreate Player 3's recreation of Player 2's recreation of Player 1's own monologue. This completes the circle so that all players have recreated someone else's performance.

How does the game end? A game of Verbatim comes to an end when all players have done a recreation of someone else's monologue. At this point the Emcee will ask the audience to vote on who they felt did the best recreation of what came before.

Pro Tip #1: Genuinely try to recreate the previous player's performance. It may seem funny to purposely put twists on what the previous player did or do the opposite, but the point of the game is to recreate the previous performance. If you purposely divert away from the original, it can spoil the game as the objective will have been lost. If you intentionally change what the other player did to either mock what they did or be creative, the audience will feel cheated as you are not attempting to recreate the previous monologue, which is the promise we gave the audience with this game.

But don't worry if you're concerned that you won't be able to demonstrate creativity. The chances are that even if you try your best, you won't be able to accurately remember the full 30 second monologue which will mean by the end of it you'll have to be embellishing and inventing ideas to fill the time.

Pro Tip #2: Have fun with recreating the previous player's performance. Copy and also emphasise their movements, their intonation, accent, moments where they stumbled on words and didn't make sense. This isn't about being mean, and in certain cases you have to tread carefully as to not offend, but your goal is to recreate their performance. If they mispronounced a word, so should you or it won't be a true recreation. If they're sat down, you should sit down.

If they have an accent or speech impediment you should use judgement as to whether an imitation would offend, but as long as you feel you don't cross a line, feel free to do your best recreation. Generally speaking if you are worried that you may offend, it may be better to play it safe in this regard, but if you are comfortable with the person and don't try to mock a characteristic of their speech you should be ok.

Pro Tip #3: If you are the first player starting the game, try to vary your monologue with changes in emotion, speech pattern, and be physical so that it gives lots of content for the following players to attempt to recreate. Avoid lots of repetition or pauses within the opening monologue as it will make it too easy for the other players to copy.

Get the audience involved!

If you think you have willing participants in the audience, you can always ask for a volunteer to take part in the game. I would suggest you do this after the first recreation. That way the audience will understand that one player recreates another, and then when you ask them to recreate the second player, they will have a sense of what they need to do.

Be very supportive of the audience member, and make it seem fun rather than there be any kind of pressure to do well. Briefly explain that it is their turn to recreate the last player and start the 30 second timer as soon as you have explained this. If you prolong the build up to them doing it, the more likely it is that they will get nervous.

There is a good chance they will hesitate at the start of the 30 seconds and also stop doing the recreation early. In both cases light heartedly inform them how long is left on the clock and encourage them to keep going.

Give them a huge round of applause at the end and ask them to wait at the side of the stage for the voting at the end of the game.

After this, get your first player to recreate everything the audience member did including any hesitations. Make sure your players always play nice, and don't mock the audience member in any way. Your audience member should always be valued above getting a cheap laugh at their expense.

Once the first player has recreated the audience member's performance you can ask the rest of the audience to vote on who did the best recreation. It is usual that the audience will vote for their fellow audience member to win the game, so you should expect this. If, somehow, they don't win, you should make sure they're given a big round of applause like they had won anyway.

31: VERBATIM DUOLOGUE

Emcee Intro Script: A team of two players are given 40 seconds to create a two-hander scene. Once this has been created a second team of two players will have 40 seconds to recreate it as exactly as they can. After this a third team of two players will have 40 seconds to recreate Team 2's recreation of the original scene. Finally, Team 1 will be given 40 seconds to recreate Team 3's recreation of Team 2's recreation of Team 1's original performance.

Challenge Style: Scene based

Players: 6

Ask the audience for: A secret that could be revealed in a relationship.

Setup: A stopwatch or egg timer would be super.

How to play the game:

#1: Team 1 are asked for perform a 40 second scene.

#2: Once they have performed it, Team 2 are given 40 seconds to recreate it as exactly as they can.

#3: Once the Team 2 has recreated the first 40 second scene, a third team of players are given 40 seconds to recreate the Team 2's recreation of Team 1's original 40 second scene.

#4: Finally, the original 2 players are given 40 seconds to recreate the third team's recreation of the recreation of their own original scene.

#5: The audience then vote on who did the best recreation of a previous scene.

Pro Tip #1: As with any other variation of Verbatim, if you are in the first version of the scene make sure the scene you create is rich with content to set a nice challenge for the following players to have to recreate.

Pro Tip #2: If you are not in the first pairing, it may be a good idea to quickly establish who in your pair is recreating which other player from the team that precedes you. If you don't, the risk is that you won't pay enough attention to the player who you need to recreate. That said, if you do end up saying lines said by the wrong character it will probably be funny – but I wouldn't recommend you do this on purpose!

Pro Tip #3: Inevitably you'll be in a pairing where you remember everything, and your scene partner remembers nothing. In this instance you'll find that they end up inventing new things which may force you to not recreate as much as you could have. My advice would be to lead the scene, if you can, and give not so subtle reminders to your scene partner to set up your own lines. This will enable the recreation to happen. The audience will see that you know what to do and that your scene partner doesn't and this will be amusing for them.

If you're the player who doesn't know what you're doing as you can't remember or wasn't paying attention...take ownership of this! Do as much as you can remember and acknowledge unapologetically when you can't. As long as you try your best with a smile on your face, the audience will forgive you...even if your scene partner doesn't.

32: COVER SONGS (VERBATIM SOLO SONGS)

Emcee Intro Script: The next improv challenge is called Cover Songs. For this challenge one performer will have to create an original 30 second song and dance routine. After this a second player will be given 30 seconds to recreate the original song and dance routine as precisely as they can. Once the second player has done this, Player 3 will have 30 seconds to recreate Player 2's recreation of the original song. Finally, Player 1 will then have 30 seconds to recreate Player 3's recreation of Player 2's recreation of Player 1's own original song and dance!

Challenge Style: Singing/Dance

Players: 3

Ask the audience for: A theme for a 30 second song.

Setup: You could either have live music or play a backing track if you want music to accompany the singing. This game can work sung a cappella if you don't have a means to have music played. If you do have music played, I would recommend having a microphone to ensure the performers can be heard singing. Additionally, a stopwatch or egg timer would be delicious.

How to play the game:

Note: The progression of Cover Songs is exactly the same as a standard game of Verbatim, but with the players performing a song instead of a monologue. Please refer to the section on the standard game of Verbatim for the detailed layout of the rules.

Pro Tip #1: If you're performing the first 30 second rendition of the song try to make sure the song has a good variety of lyrics and not too many 'la la las' or repeated phrases. Whilst these may be regular features of songs normally, it will make this game too easy for the following players to be able to recreate the song. Keep in mind that the audience will have to sit through 4 versions of the same song, so if the first one is just 30 seconds of 'la la las' you're forcing the audience to have to watch that another three times over!

Pro Tip #2: Keep in mind that not all performers may be able to sing to the same standard...and use that to hilarious effect! If you start off with your best singer and they can include all kinds of held notes, fast raps, and vocal gymnastics they will be setting the table for the rest of the players to have to imitate that skill. And by the time the best singer has to recreate a bad performance, they won't be allowed to fix the song – the good singer will have to do their best bad singing which will be to hilarious effect.

Pro Tip #3: In complete contradiction of the previous tip, if you have a really good singer who is tasked with recreating a bad singer they could purposely take the bad version and clean it up to still be recognisable but also sound really good. This would likely get a positive reaction from the audience even if it is not a close recreation.

33: VERBATIM DUET

Brief Description:

This game is essentially the same as Cover Songs but played with teams of two players performing a duet. The song they create could be extended to 45 seconds to give more time for turn taking in the singing, but other than this change, the game follows the same principals as other versions of Verbatim covered in this book.

34: MOVIE DIRECTOR

Emcee Intro Script: This next game is called Movie Director! And in this game one of our performers is going to play a Movie Director, and the others are going to play as actors in a film the director is making.

The actors are going to create a scene, and every so often the Director will call 'Cut' and give a new direction for the actors to do another take of the same scene. This will happen many times until we get "the perfect take."

Challenge Style: Scene based

Players: 3+

Ask the audience for: A name for a fictional Hollywood blockbuster.

How to play the game:

#1: The players create a scene from this fictional Hollywood blockbuster that lasts about a minute or two.

#2: The Director calls 'Cut' and enters the scene. They express their feelings on the take that just happened and give a new direction for how the scene should be performed differently. Once the actors have given this, the director exits the stage and calls 'Take 2. Action!'

#3: The original scene is recreated with changes to reflect the director's suggestions. As examples, the Director could suggest the players do the scene again in the style of a western, or that one player changes their character to be a child.

#4: Once the scene has been repeated with the new direction, the director can once again call 'Cut' to stop the scene. They will then give another new direction for the next take, and this process repeats several times over with new directions.

How does the game end? The directing character can end it by calling cut and declaring 'that's a wrap'. Or the scene can be ended by the Emcee when it is time to move on to something else in the show.

Pro Tip #1: If you are the directing character you can play around with your characterisation. Are you a nice director, or extremely strict?

Pro Tip #2: If you are a performer in the scene being repeated, try to make sure that the scene follows the same basic beats every time. The new direction will alter how you do it, but the aim of this game is to adjust the delivery of the scene, and not to create a completely different one from scratch.

35: ONE MINUTE REMAKE

Emcee Intro Script: Spoiler alert! This next game may contain spoilers for films you have not seen yet, because we're going to play One Minute Remake! Our performers will condense entire movies into just one minute complete with award winning speeches, explosive action sequences and heart-breaking drama.

Challenge Style: Scene based

Players: 1+

Ask the audience for: Well-known movies.

Setup: It would be useful to have a timer for this game, but this doesn't have to be strict and the Emcee could allow the performer to go slightly over or under to complete their scene.

How to play the game:

#1: The performer(s) will get one minute to recreate entire movies. This includes the whole plot, playing multiple characters and the most famous lines and moments.

The story they create should be more than just a single scene from the movie. The idea is to recreate the entire story - beginning, middle and end.

How does the game end? The scene should be ended by the performer(s), but the Emcee can call time on it if it's going on for too long.

Pro Tip #1: If you don't know the film at all you can say to the Emcee and it may be possible to take an alternative suggestion. Alternatively, you could create a one minute version of the movie based solely on your limited knowledge of it, even if all you know is the title.

Pro Tip #2: Depending how many players are involved in the game (and it could just be one) it is probable that you may have to play multiple parts. If so, do what you can to make the characterisations distinct from one another through voice and physicality. This may be more difficult if you are recreating a film where the original characters and the actors playing them aren't very distinct from one another. If this is the case all you can do is your best to find ways to make them feel unique.

One way you could do this would be to make a bold physicality choice early in the game to establish how similar characters are presented differently. For example if you were recreating 'The Lord of the Rings' and were playing multiple hobbits you could decide that Sam always slouches, that Pippin always scratches himself nervously, that Merry does a little jig every time he speaks and Frodo always has his sword up ready to fight. The audience would quickly recognise these characteristics as meaning you are playing that specific character.

SECTION 5: TWO BECOME ONE

To quote the song by the Spice Girls 'Come a little bit closer baby, get it on, get it on,
'Cause tonight is the night when two become one.'

The games in this section all focus on two or more players combining their efforts to create a whole which is greater than the sum of its parts.

With creative costuming, you can combine to become a strange two headed person in a Dreaded Gemini or Libra scene.

36: THREE HEADED EXPERT

Emcee Intro Script: In a game of Three Headed Expert, three players will put their heads together to become a strange three headed person. Each of the three heads will speak one word at a time. For clarity, the three players are working together to play as one character. They will then answer questions from a fourth single headed player.

Challenge Style: Scene based/Interview

Players: 4

Ask the audience for: What the three headed character is an expert of.

Setup: The three players working together as the 3 headed expert should all stand or sit together and mimic or cannon each other's behaviour. The interviewing player should be set separately from the 3 headed expert so there is no confusion whether they are part of the multiple headed character.

How to play the game:

#1: The interviewing character will ask questions to the 3 headed expert character and lead the scene.

#2: The performers playing the 3 headed character speak one word at a time. This goes in the order: Stage Right Head, Middle Head, Stage Left Head and loops in this order for as long as the length of the line of dialogue.

For more info on this technique including how to establish who should speak when and understanding stage left/right see the pro tips below.

#3: The body language displayed by the 3 headed character usually mimics one another – that is to say each of the three performers playing that one role copy any significant movements any of the players do.

How does the game end?

The scene ends when the interviewing character brings the interview to a natural close.

Pro Tip #1: The three headed character should always be referred to as an individual. This means the three players performing as the 3 headed expert will refer to themselves as 'I' rather than 'we' and 'mine' rather than 'ours'.

Pro Tip #2: With the 3 headed character you can sometimes get confused as to which player should speak next. For example, if the middle head was the last to speak of the three heads and then the interviewer asks a question which of the heads should say the next word? The middle one again? The left one? Or the right one? And whose left or right? The performers or the audience? See how confusing this can get? Don't worry, here's the way to solve this problem:

With the three headed character you want to assign them as Stage Right Head, Middle Head and Stage Left Head. Stage Right Head will be the lead head and will always start new lines of dialogue. This will prevent any confusion and stop the risk of two performers both coming in to start a new line at the same time.

As the saying goes, three heads are better than two...

In case you're not sure, here's how to understand which is stage left and which is stage right.

To do this stand on stage facing directly to the audience. As you face the audience the direction to your right is...stage right. And the direction to your left is therefore unsurprisingly stage left.

The reason this can get confusing is because if you were watching the show as the audience member, stage right would appear to be the left side of the stage...but as this is the acting world we're using the acting terms and stage right is always the actor's right as they are facing the audience.

Pro Tip #3: If you are the interviewer you can have fun with the questions you ask the 3 headed character. Ask them to sing a song or recite a poem and the audience will be aware that you are giving them a hard challenge to complete. Win or lose the audience will usually find their efforts commendable and funny.

37: THE DREADED GEMINI SCENE

Emcee Intro Script: In the Dreaded Gemini Scene, teams of two players will have to perform as a single strange two headed character. They achieve this by standing next to each other, moving together and speaking where each head takes turns to talk one word at a time.

Challenge Style: Scene based/Language challenge/Physical

Players: 4-6

Ask the audience for: A type of relationship between people.

Setup: This scene can be achieved simply by players standing side by side next to each other close enough that they can hold an arm over the shoulder of each other, but for the most visual effect, this scene is enhanced with specially created two headed costumes. This can be two T-shirts stitched together into one garment, and three-legged trousers.

How to play the game:

#1: Two players work together to create a single character. This is achieved by standing next to each other and moving together as if they are one person. Dialogue should be spoken one word at a time taking turns between each head. Each actor in the two person team will only have one hand available as part of the two headed character: the stage right head will have access to use their right hand whilst the stage left character will have their left hand available.

How does the game end?

This game ends when the Emcee feels the scene has run its course or it reaches a satisfying end point.

Pro Tip #1: To ensure that there is minimal confusion of which player on each team should start new lines of dialogue, follow this rule of thumb:

The stage right player on a team will always be the first head to speak. To understand which player this is, it would be the player in a team stood to the right as both players face the audience.

Pro Tip #2: Keep your two headed characters active and busy on stage. The challenge of this scene is for two actors to perform in sync as one, and the more you attempt to move around the stage and interact with each other the more visually impressive it will be for the audience. That isn't to say to move around for the sake of it but try to keep things interesting.

Pro Tip #3: To enhance the presentation that each two-player team is playing as one character, try things with your hands as a pair such as clapping each other's hands, scratching each other's chins or putting up your dukes ready for fisticuffs that demonstrate that each hand is part of the same character.

38: THE LIBRA SCENE

Brief Description of the Game: The Libra Scene is a similar game to The Dreaded Gemini Scene in its format and presentation, but with a key major difference as detailed below.

Emcee Intro Script: Next up we are going to have a Libra Scene! In a Libra Scene, teams of two players will have to work together to perform as a single strange two headed character. They achieve this by standing next to each other, moving together and speaking where both heads will say the same words at the same time.

Challenge Style: Scene based/Language challenge/Physical

Players: 4-6

Ask the audience for: A type of relationship between people.

Setup: Like the Dreaded Gemini Scene, players should stand next to each other and if possible, wear specially created two headed costumes.

How to play the game:

#1: Two players work together as a team to create a single character. This is achieved by standing next to each other and moving together as if they are one person. When it comes to dialogue the goal is for both players on a team to say the exact same words at the exact same time.

How does the game end?

This game ends when the Emcee feels the scene reaches a satisfying end point.

Pro Tip #1: In order for two players to be able to say the exact same words at the exact same time, I would recommend that speech be slower than normal at times. This will allow both players working together to get a sense of what words are being said and from here you will be able to anticipate what sentences are being formed. If you are both on the same page it should be possible to slightly speed up the speech when you're confident that you are both now saying the same sentence.

Pro Tip #2: Exactly as with a Gemini Scene. Make sure you keep your two headed characters active and busy on stage. The scene will seem dull if you just stand there and talk. Moving around and doing things in your pairs will help keep the scene visually interesting and physical actions will also help inspire new ways to drive the story forwards.

Why is this game called a Libra Scene? As a similar format to a Gemini scene it seemed fitting to give it another astrological name. And whilst the Gemini name represents the dual nature of a personality, Libra being represented by scales made sense for this game where there is balance between two players performing in sync with one another.

39: TABLEAU TURMOIL

Emcee Intro Script: In Tableau Turmoil two teams will compete to make pictures of various things using nothing but their bodies. The players will have to work in their teams to create complex images by combining as one.

Challenge Style: Physical Theatre

Players: 4-8 split into teams

Ask the audience for: Suggestions of anything that they could make a picture of – buildings, landmarks, emotions, people, animals, sports etc etc.

Setup: You will need enough space for two teams to create elaborate ideas. Also ensure that there is enough gap between the teams so their creations don't blur into one another.

How to play the game:

#1: Working as a team, you use your body to create shapes to form pictures or scenes based on audience suggestions.

#2: The Emcee will announce what the picture you should make is and give a 5 second count down for each tableau to be created.

#3: The pictures you create should not include movement, speech or sound effects.

#4: Once the team have made their pictures the Emcee can ask the audience which team they felt did the better job and vote for their favourite.

How does the game end?

This game could be played for a set number of rounds – such as a best of 10 rounds.

Playing house...

Pro Tip #1: Ideally the pictures your team create should be self-explanatory, and not require you to explain what the various elements mean to the audience. This said, don't be afraid to create slightly abstract interpretations of the themes as these may win over the audience. If for example the Emcee tasks you with creating a tableau of 'Home' this could mean you make a picture of a house. Alternatively, you could make a picture showing a family in the sense of family representing home.

Pro Tip #2: Cheat to Win. You may get away with very minor movements or sound effects at the Emcee's discretion, or if it goes down well with the audience. Examples of these could include waving your fingers to represent fire, a slight motion in your body to represent that you are floating in water, or a adding a hum to represent bees or elevator music. If you push these limits on movement/sound too much you simply won't be playing this game anymore.

40: HELPING HANDS

Emcee Intro Script: A classic improv game for you now. Let's play Helping Hands! The way this works is that one of the improvisers is going to play a character, but they will not be able to use their own hands and arms to perform the scene. Instead a second performer is going to stand behind them and provide the arms for the character. We will also provide several interesting props for the character to interact with.

Challenge Style: Scene based/Physical

Players: 2+

Ask the audience for: N/A. The scene is usually centred around a theme dictated by the props available.

Setup: For this game it would be useful to have many props laid out on a table for the person using their hands to be able to interact with. Having actual food that can be eaten and made a mess with can also be fun in this game.

Examples of useful props for this game:

- Food that can really be consumed
- Cold drinks
- Hats
- Glasses
- Books
- Painting/drawing items
- Toothbrush

Examples of props that you shouldn't use in this game:

- Knives
- Scissors
- Matches
- Live alligators
- Boiling water
- Needles
- Pin badges

How to play the game:

#1: Player 1 stands with their arms tucked behind their backs. Player 1 will be the face, body and voice of a character.

#2: Player 2 stands directly behind Player 1 and tucks their arms through Player 1's arms to give the impression that Player 2's arms are actually the arms of Player 1. Player 2 is the arms of Player 1's character.

#3: Working together, Player 1 and 2 create a character where Player 1 speaks and sets up ideas of what they want Player 2 to do with the character's hands.

Likewise, Player 2 can independently do things with their hands which Player 1 can respond to verbally. In this sense neither player is the leader, and they both bounce off and respond to each other.

#4: This game is frequently played by three players where Player 1 is the body, face and voice of a character and Player 2 is the same character's arms. Player 3 would then be a separate character who is interacting with the character played by Players 1 and 2.

A 2-player version of this game is possible where the scenario is that Player 1 would be giving some kind of presentation to the audience, thus not needing a third player for them to interact with.

A 4-player version of this game would see Players 1 and 2 as the body/arms of the first character and Players 3 and 4 being the second character.

How does the game end? The Emcee will end this scene when the players have reached a suitable ending point in the scene.

Pro Tip #1: Player 1 can slightly break the fourth wall and acknowledge the audience at times. This can show the actor's attitude to what Player 2 is doing with their hands to great comedic effect. This is based around the logic that the audience will enjoy knowing that this isn't the most comfortable scenario for the player to be in. This shouldn't be overdone, but is fun for the audience to watch.

Pro Tip #2: Player 2 can purposely go against what Player 1 has said. By playing against expectations you can make these 'alien hands' disobey the rest of their body and do things which clearly Player 1 doesn't want them to do.

41: HUMAN PUPPETS

Emcee Intro Script: Next up our performers are going to become Human Puppets where they perform a scene where they can only move their bodies if volunteers from the audience physically move them as if they were puppeteers.

Challenge Style: Scene based/Physical

Players: 2 players + 2 audience members

Ask the audience for:

#1: 2 volunteers to be the puppeteers.

#2: A scenario such as a task you may need to do that has a time limit.

How to play the game:

#1: The two performers cannot move in the scene unless they are moved physically by the volunteers from the audience. The only exceptions are that the performers are allowed to talk, blink and breath. Heart beats are also allowed at the Emcee's discretion.

#2: The volunteers should be assigned to a player each. It shouldn't be that the audience members can swap between each player.

#3: Make it clear to the audience members that they need to be gentle with the performers, and not to touch the players inappropriately. This is important to say, but should be done in a light hearted way so not to make anyone uncomfortable.

How does the game end? The game ends at the Emcee's discretion.

Pro Tip #1: Players should use their dialogue to justify any movements the volunteer makes them do.

Pro tip #2: Players can lead the action by announcing they intend to do a physical action. This will give a hint to the volunteer that they would like to be moved in a certain way.

Either the volunteer will pick up on your hint and make you do it, or they won't make you do it in which case you can play off the fact that you changed your mind, lied etc. But be careful that it doesn't become that you just give instructions to your volunteer of what you want your character to do. Let them take control at least as much if not more than yourself.

Pro Tip #3: Don't forget what the scene is about, and always drive the story forward. It can be easy with this game to lose a sense of the scenario and just focus on the physical actions that the audience member is making you do. Always try to tie the physical actions back to the story you are telling.

SECTION 6: LISTEN VERY CAREFULLY, I SHALL SAY THIS ONLY ONCE

In the games that follow you will be tasked to speak without saying any word more than once. According to a quick Google search (as I do with any research in this book) there are 273,000 words in the English language. So, this should be easy right?

'Did you know that there are 50 Eskimo words for snow? Number 1...'

42: JUST A MINUTE

Emcee Intro Script: The next challenge is Just a Minute. As heard over the radio waves for over fifty years, this is a timed game, with a 60 second time limit! One performer will start the game and be given the opportunity to speak for just a minute without hesitation, repetition or deviation. If another player notices that they break any of these rules they can buzz in and the timer will stop. If they have correctly identified a broken rule, they can take over performing.

Whoever is speaking at the end of the 60 seconds wins the round, and points will also be awards for correct challenges of when other players have broken the rules.

Challenge Style: Monologue

Players: 1 player performs at a time. Additional players can challenge and take over the speech.

Ask the audience for:

A subject to be discussed by the player.

Setup: You will need some kind of timer or stopwatch for this game.

How to play the game:

#1: Hesitation. Whilst performing a player is not allowed to use extended or dramatic pauses or say non words such as 'eerrrr' or 'ummmm'. Your speed of speech may also count as hesitation if you draw words out for too long or have a terribly slow delivery which continually borders the line of an extended pause. In these instances, it will be up to the Emcee's discretion.

#2: Repetition. In Just a Minute, you are not allowed to repeat any words whilst performing...although there are two exceptions.

Firstly, you can repeat a word if it is part of the topic you have been challenged to discuss.

For example, if you are supposed to talk about 'cheese', you can repeat the word cheese a few times, although not excessively. So, you couldn't use up the minute saying 'Cheese, cheese, cheese, cheese, cheese.'

Nor could you get away with saying 'I love cheese, because cheese is the best, and say cheese when having my photo with a block of cheese.' This would still be seen as excessive. You could probably get away with using the subject word 4-5 times across an entire minute, but not in quick succession. The Emcee will make the judgement call if a player has challenged you on excessive repetition of the subject word.

Secondly, depending on the Emcee's discretion you may be allowed to repeat small words such as I, A, and, the, of and as. Again, if you were to use any of these excessively you can expect the Emcee to not allow it.

#3: Deviation: In Just a Minute there is the no deviation rule. This means that if you are tasked with talking about the subject of cheese, you should make sure everything you say relates to the subject of cheese and doesn't stray too far off.

If you're supposed to talk about cheese and after 20 seconds all you've spoken about is football, this would be deviation. If however you tell a story of when you were a child and were given a football made of cheese and played against a team of mice...it wouldn't be deviation as long as you continually keep the theme of cheese relevant to the story.

#4: A nonperforming player can buzz in or call 'freeze' to interrupt a performing player. They should only do this to make a challenge based on the above three rules, but this can also be used for a comedic opportunity. This can include making a humorous observation on what the performing player is saying. In Just a Minute the Emcee may decide to give you a bonus point for doing this, but I would recommend doing this sparingly as it disrupts the flow of the game.

#5: If a nonperforming player makes an incorrect challenge within the rules, the performing player gets to continue speaking. This does not reset the words they have said, and they can still be challenged on repetition for repeating a word after resuming.

#6: If a player is correctly challenged, but later takes over the subject again, they do get a clean slate of words to start from scratch with. This is because keeping track of words between different players speaking would be too confusing.

How does the game end?

Just a Minute ends at the end of the one-minute time limit. Multiple rounds can be played and how many is up to you.

Pro Tip #1: Lists are your friend! 'I bought a coat and it had patches of red, blue, green, yellow, brown, black, white...' This may seem like it is cheating, but it isn't! As long as the list is relevant to the subject and doesn't cross into deviation it's ok to do. However, if you do this too often the audience may turn on you, and the Emcee may side against you...on the grounds of 'repetition of lists'.

Also keep in mind that while lists don't break the rules, they can make the game seem too easy and if done too much will make the game less appealing to audiences.

Pro Tip #2: Find multiple ways of saying the same thing.

You're not allowed to repeat words, but can say variations of the same word such as:

- 'I love cheeses, especially cheesy cheese.'

You may also be able to get away with slightly made up versions of real words such as:

- 'I ate so much cheese, I'm now fully cheesed. It was a cheese-tastic day.'

This will be up to the kindness of the other players, audience and the Emcee's discretion.

You can also use different words that say the same thing such as:

- 'I love cheese. Especially cheddar. Put that dairy block in my mouth and it's gone!'

Or to give a non-cheese example, here's an example if you had to talk about William Shakespeare:

- 'Good old Shakespeare! The Bard wrote many plays. My favourite of William's scripts is The Tempest. It truly was Bill's best work! Billy also did great tragedies. Although his father wasn't a fan. "This sad book you've written ain't my cuppa tea, Shakesy" as Mr Shakes Snr would call him.'

See how many different ways it was possible to refer to both William Shakespeare and his plays without any repeated words?

43: EXTREME MONOLOGUE

Emcee Intro Script: The next challenge is the Extreme Monologue, which is a timed game, with a 90 second time limit! One performer will start the game and be given the opportunity to perform a monologue with the goal of keeping it going until the time limit runs out without repetition, hesitation and devastation.

There are three rules they are not allowed to break. Rule one: No repetition. They are not allowed to repeat any words whatsoever. This includes even very small words such as I, the and 'and'.

Rule two. No hesitation. Players are not allowed to hesitate which we count as extended pauses or saying non words such as 'errrr' or 'ummm'.

Rule three. No devastation. If you don't like the first two rules...tough. This is a harsh game.

If the player breaks any of these rules the other performers and even the audience can call 'Freeze' to pause the monologue. If another player has correctly identified that a rule has been broken, they are given the opportunity to take over performing the monologue, with the same rules applying to them. Whoever is in control of the monologue at the end of 90 seconds wins the round.

Challenge Style: Monologue/Audience Participation

Players: 1 player performs at a time. Additional players can challenge and take over the monologue.

Ask the audience for:

#1: Characters from fiction/people from history.

#2: Things the characters are happy/sad about, a secret they have, a situation they are in etc.

Setup: You will need a timer for this game. Unfortunately, a sundial simply won't cut it.

How to play the game:

#1: No repetition whatsoever! Unlike a game of Just a Minute, in an Extreme Monologue you are not allowed to repeat any words whatsoever. This includes any subjects you may have been tasked with discussing and small words such as I, a, on, the, if and in. It may seem harsh, and as if it makes the game impossible to play, but that is the game!

#2: No hesitation. This counts as extended pauses or saying non words such as 'errr' or 'ummmm'.

#3: No devastation. Don't like how harsh this game feels compared to regular Just a Minute? Hard cheese! No whinging, no whining allowed. This is a jokey rule, but as this is an extreme version of Just a Minute we felt it proper to include an equivalent to the no deviation rule. Which incidentally isn't a named rule for an Extreme Monologue...and here's why:

Why no Deviation rule?

Unlike Just a Minute in which players are effectively themselves talking about a subject, in an Extreme Monologue the performers are playing the part of a character, and performing a monologue based on an emotion or specific scenario.

As such we feel it would be too limiting for the performer to restrict how far off of the starting point a monologue can go. This is because a primary aim of improvisation that we encourage is to always drive the story forwards. So, if you start your monologue in a supermarket, and within 20 seconds find your character is now at the bottom of the ocean...great!

A scene that doesn't go anywhere because you're trying not to deviate from the subject isn't as fun as a scene that has endless possibilities.

#4: If a nonperforming player calls 'freeze' and gives an incorrect challenge, the player who was interrupted may continue their monologue. Note that this does not reset the monologue and any words they had previously said can be held against them should they say them again after the monologue restarts.

#5: If Player 1 is correctly challenged by Player 2, but later Player 1 challenges Player 2 and retakes control of the monologue, Player 1 will be gifted a clean slate. This means that the words they said during their previous attempt won't be held against them should they resay a word one time in the new attempt.

How does the game end?

An Extreme Monologue ends once the 90 second time limit for the monologue has been reached. Whoever is speaking when the time runs out wins the game.

Pro Tip #1: Don't talk about the character – be the character! Sometimes a player may be given a character such as Robin Hood, and when they start the game may say something like 'Robin Hood is a character who falls in love with Maid Marian...' Whilst that sentence doesn't break any of the rules listed above, the player has made the mistake of talking about the character rather than talking as if they are the character.

This game is an opportunity to play as the character, so don't waste it by giving the audience a history lesson about the character instead.

Pro Tip #2: If you don't know who the character you are playing is, I would recommend just making a big choice in terms of voice and physicality and do something anyway. If you acknowledge or make it obvious that you don't know who your character is the audience will enjoy your ploughing on regardless.

Pro Tip #3: As with Just a Minute lists are your friend in this version of the game. More so in fact as a good list will help you avoid the small words that aren't allowed in an Extreme Monologue...if you can get away with performing a list without the audience turning on you that is! Just don't fall into the noob list trap and say something like 'It was red and blue and green and yellow...' If you add 'and' between every word, you'll have failed the challenge!

44: EXTREME MONOLOGUE ENDURANCE

Brief Description of the Game:

An Extreme Monologue Endurance works basically the same as a regular Extreme Monologue, but with a slight difference of how it's competed. Please refer to the section on the regular Extreme Monologue to understand how the game is played, so you will understand the following differences.

Instead of there being a 90 second time limit to the monologue, the goal is now for each performer to perform a monologue and keep it going for as long as possible without breaking the rules of Repetition, Hesitation or Devastation.

If another performer notices that any of these rules have been broken, they can call 'Freeze' and that will be the end of the monologue.

After a correct challenge, a new player will attempt to do a monologue and keep it going for as long as they can until they are correctly challenged.

This process continues until every player has attempted a monologue and the winner is the player who performed the longest monologue without breaking the rules.

45: TAG TEAM EXTREME MONOLOGUE

Emcee Intro Script: Teams of two players will attempt to perform monologues where each player in a team can speak one word at a time. As a team they will perform as if they are a single two headed character and attempt to keep the monologue going for 90 seconds which is the time limit for the game.

There are two rules they cannot break which are that as a team they are not allowed to repeat any words whatsoever, and they are not allowed to hesitate, which we count as saying non words such as 'errr' or 'ummm' or leaving extended pauses between words.

If a team breaks either of these rules, another team can call 'Freeze' and if they have made a correct challenge, they can take over the monologue. Whichever team is in control of the monologue at the end of 90 seconds wins the game and advances onto a 1 on 1 face off playing by standard Extreme Monologue rules *(see the rules of Extreme Monologue for this).*

Challenge Style: Monologue

Players: 2+

Ask the audience for: A character from fiction or history and something for them to be happy about.

Setup: You will need to have a stopwatch or timer.

How to play the game:

#1: Players are put into teams of two.

#2: A team will attempt to perform a monologue where the players in a team can only speak one word at a time as if they are all the same character.

#3: As a team, the players are not allowed to repeat any words whatsoever. This means that one of the players on the team cannot say a word that their partner has already said.

#4: As a team no player is allowed to hesitate, which is defined as leaving extended pauses between words or saying non words such as 'errr' or 'ummm'.

Note that even though two players are taking turns to say one word at a time each they should speak as fast in this game as if it was one person speaking. Don't allow extra pauses because two people are playing together.

How does the game end?

This game ends at the end of the 90 second time limit on the monologue.

Pro Tip #1: Remember that you're performing a monologue, so try to keep your energy, volume and delivery at a similar level as your team mate so that it flows well.

46: EXTREME SOLO (SINGING)

Brief Description: An Extreme Solo is basically the same as an Extreme Monologue, except instead of performing a monologue, the players are performing a made-up song. Please refer to the rules of the Extreme Monologue game but see the below additional information to highlight the differences of this game.

Emcee Intro Script: In an Extreme Solo, each player will attempt to sing a song for as long as possible without repeating any words whatsoever or leaving extended pauses between lyrics. We also limit how many notes can be held for long periods before we count that as a hesitation. If they break either of these rules another player can call 'Freeze' and if they have correctly identified a broken rule the song will end and the time the song lasted will be recorded. Whichever player can keep their song going for the longest wins.

Challenge Style: Singing

Players: 2+

Ask the audience for: The name of a made-up song.

Setup: This can be sung with or without music, and with or without microphones depending on what you have available.

How to play the game:

Additional Rule: Held notes. If a player attempts to keep their song going with notes held for long periods of time, this can be held against them as both a hesitation and a repetition of the note. This can be left up to the Emcee's discretion as held notes can be a positive feature of singing, but too much repetition of this will affect the challenge of the game and lose the audience.

Held notes can actually make the game too easy and if this happens too much will cause the audience to lose interest. Keep the song flowing and the lyrics diverse to add to the challenge.

Pro Tip #1: Songs lend themselves to figurative language. Metaphors and symbolism will allow you to describe the same thing in many different ways without repeating words.

SECTION 7: SPECIFIC GOALS

The following collection of games are all structurally siblings to one another. They see you do a scene with a very specific goal, which usually relates to something you must or must not do.

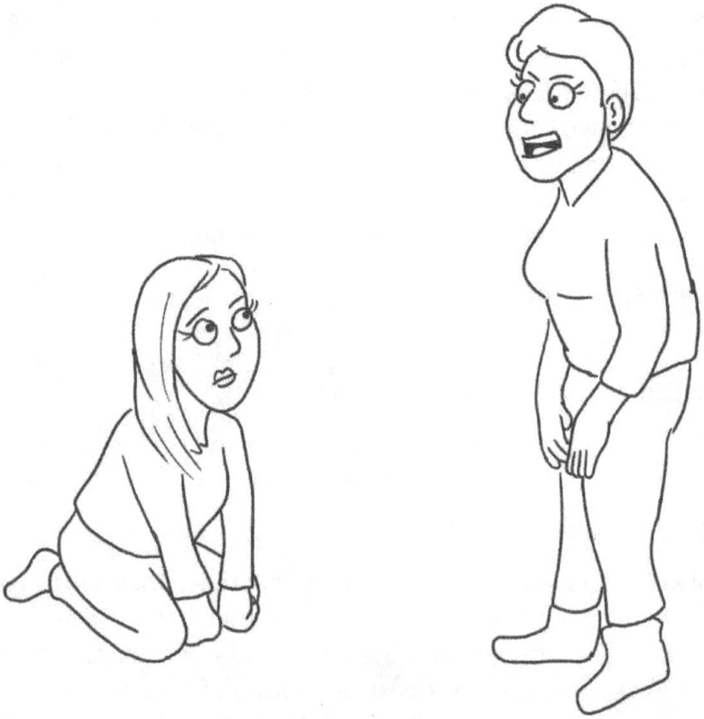

If you're in a scene and can't use your feet, you may find yourself looking up to your scene partner.

47: ALLITERATION ANARCHY

Emcee Intro Script: Our next challenge is called Alliteration Anarchy. The way it works is our performers will act out a scene, and whilst they can say any words they like, they have a goal.

Each of the performers will be assigned a letter of the alphabet, and as much as possible they need to begin as many of the words as they individually say with the letter they have been assigned. At the end of the scene you will vote who you felt made the best creative use of their letter.

Challenge Style: Scene based

Players: 2-5 (3 recommended)

Ask the audience for:

#1: A suggestion for a scenario.

#2: Letters of the alphabet which are then assigned to each player.

How to play the game:

#1: Before the scene begins the Emcee assigns each player with a letter of the alphabet.

#2: Whilst each player can say any words they like, they have the goal of beginning as many of their words as possible with the letter they have been assigned.

How does the game end?

Alliteration Anarchy ends when the Emcee feels the scene has run its course or reached a natural conclusion.

Pro Tip #1: Don't forget you ARE allowed to say words that don't begin with your individually assigned letter. So, for example if you were assigned the letter 'S' you could say:

Player 1: Sorry Sarah, I saw someone screaming from the top of their lungs. The silly sausage.

Pro Tip #2: Don't be afraid to emphasise the beginning sound of the words you say that start with your assigned letter. Let's look at the previous example sentence now written to show how you might emphasise the beginning letter.

Player 1: Sssorry Sssarah, I Sssaw Sssomeone Ssscreaming from the top of their lungs. The Sssilly Sssausage.

Pro Tip #3: The more difficult letters are the obvious ones – Q, J, Z, X and K. With these letters do what you can, but know that if you get them, you'll have a tougher time of things, so creativity and humour will be key.

For example, you could use an accent to substitute a tough letter for an easier one. A 'Z' can be used instead of a 'Th' sound so the sentence 'This is the theatre' could be pronounced as 'Zis is ze zeatre.'

You can also apply this same method to easier letters such as faking a speech impediment on words beginning with 'R' if you are assigned the letter 'W'. This would allow sentences such as:

'I'm weally weally worried that Wachel, Wobin and Webecca are wet fwom the wain. It's been waining wet water all week.'

48: BODY LANGUAGE

Emcee Intro Script: This next challenge is called Body Language. Our performers will each be assigned a body part which they will then have to use as creatively as they can throughout the scene. After the scene has finished, we will have a vote on who made the best creative use of their body part.

Challenge Style: Scene based/Physical

Players: 2-5 (3 recommended)

Ask the audience for:

#1: A scenario such as a place of work.

#2: A body part which will be assigned to each player.

Note: If an audience member suggests a body part which the player would not be comfortable basing their performance around, the player has the power to veto the suggestion. The Emcee should always check in to make sure a player is happy with the body part they are being asked to use, and a player can say no at any time.

How to play the game:

#1: Each player is assigned a body part by the audience.

#2: The goal is to use the body part you have been assigned as creatively as you can throughout the scene.

How does the game end?

Once the scene is over the audience vote on which player they felt used their assigned body part most creatively.

Pro Tip #1: Try to really emphasise the body part you have been assigned but do so in ways that make sense to the scenario. If you've been assigned your hands, then find opportunities to clap, shake other players hands, point at things etc.

Pro Tip #2: Don't just wiggle and wave the body part you've been assigned all over the place without good reason. To do so will just be confusing for the audience and lose their interest.

Pro Tip #3: This scene lends itself to heightened physical performances, but don't be afraid to throw in word play that relates to the body part you have been assigned.

Pro Tip #4: It's very possible that the audience will assign you a body part that is either internal (such as your liver) or something you can't really move independently (such as your toenails or skin) If you have a tricky body part like these, try to think creatively about how the body part could be relevant. You can emphasise a liver by coming on stage and drinking heavily, or just acknowledging an internal injury.

As another example if you were given 'brain' you could play your character as super smart or as a zombie that is obsessed with eating brains.

49: IMMOBILISE

Emcee Intro Script: We will now play a round of Immobilise. The way it works is that the improvisers will perform a scene, but each of them will be assigned a body part they are not allowed to use during their performance. At all. After the scene has ended, we will ask you to vote on who you feel performed best with their limitation.

Challenge Style: Scene based

Players: 2-5 (3 recommended)

Ask the audience for:

#1: A scenario such as a mystery that needs to be solved.

#2: Body parts which will be assigned to each player.

How to play the game:

#1: In Immobilise each player is assigned a body part which they are not allowed to use throughout the scene.

How does the game end?

After the scene is over the audience vote on which player gave the most creative performance in spite of the body part they were not allowed to use.

Pro Tip #1: Don't cheat. If you're told you cannot use your head that means you can't talk and should probably shut your eyes to highlight that the functions of your head are now off limits. If you're told you can't use your legs don't just stand there – instead fall to the floor and drag yourself along like a zombie.

Likewise, if you're told you can't use your heart immediately collapse and stay dead throughout the scene. The audience want to see the actors struggle, and this is the ultimate game of restrictions to make the actors struggle.

Pro Tip #2: Do cheat. If you're told you can't use your brain, then be clever about it! Announce yourself as the President or give yourself a job title like schoolteacher etc to ironically show you are not using your brain.

Pro Tip #3: Set yourself up for failure. If you can't use a body part, announce you are going to do something that would normally require that body part.

For example if you can't use your legs, try saying: 'Quick run for it!' Even though it's obvious you can't.

50: SELF CONTROL

Emcee Intro Script: Our next game is Self Control. In this game each player will be assigned an emotion which they have to use as creatively as they can within the scene they create. After the scene is done you will vote on who you felt demonstrated the most self control...or lack thereof.

Challenge Style: Scene based

Players: 3-5

Ask the audience for:

#1: A scenario such as a reason for a family gathering.

#2: An emotion to be assigned to each player.

How to play the game:

#1: Every player in the scene is assigned an emotion which they have to make the best creative use of as they can.

How does the game end? The Emcee chooses a good point to end the scene if it hasn't reached a natural conclusion. At this point the Emcee then asks the audience to vote on who they felt made the best use of the emotion they were assigned.

Pro Tip #1: Use different levels of the emotion which you have been assigned. Don't always have it at level 10. Show signs of you bringing it under control and then let it flare up.

Pro Tip #2: Does something from the scenario or another player's actions trigger your emotion? Try to make your character's emotions relevant to the scene you are in. If another player's emotion is anger and yours is love, maybe you love it when they get angry. Look for opportunities to bounce off each other.

51: SENSELESS

Emcee Intro Script: Our next game is senseless...and it's also called Senseless too. The way it works is our performers are each going to be assigned a sense which they are not allowed to use in the scene. After the scene is completed the audience will vote on who did the best with their limitation.

Challenge Style: Scene based

Players: 2-5

Ask the audience for:

#1: A scenario such as a type of holiday.

#2: Each player needs to be assigned a sense they cannot use in the scene. These can include senses such as sight, hearing, smell, taste and touch, or more elaborate ideas such as a sense of style, sense of balance or sense of humour.

How to play the game:

#1: The players perform the scene whilst highlighting the absence of their particular sense. This can be through dialogue, or physicality.

How does the game end? Once the Emcee feels the scene has run its course, they can end the scene. They will then ask the audience to vote on who did best with their individual sensory limitation.

Pro Tip #1: You should look for opportunities within the scenario that would normally require you to use your missing sense. You will then be able to draw attention to the fact that you cannot use that sense as it is missing.

52: EVERY SENTENCE MUST

Emcee Intro Script: One of our more challenging games, we will now play Every Sentence Must. In this game our performers will create a scene with the challenge that every time a performer says a line of dialogue...every sentence must...include a word from a selected category.

The category for this game is...*(insert category here as decided by the Emcee)*

Challenge Style: Scene based, Word Play

Players: 2-5

Ask the audience for:

A scenario such as an outdoor activity.

Suggested Categories:

- Foods
- Fruits and Vegetables
- Movie Titles
- Book Titles
- Song Titles
- Electrical goods
- Clothes
- Drinks
- Body Parts
- Geographical locations

Why is it not recommended for the audience to suggest the category?

I don't recommend you allow the audience to suggest the category as not every category will provide as rich a pool of words as the suggested ones in this guide. For example, if you asked the audience to suggest a category they could suggest something such as names of supermarkets. On the surface this may sound reasonable, but only gives you maybe 20 common terms you could potentially use. And because all the words would be names, they don't really lend themselves that easily to repurposing as other things.

How to play the game:

#1: Every time a player says a new line of dialogue, it must include a word from the category the Emcee stated before the game began.

How does the game end?

Don't expect this to be a very long lasting game. It should be ended by the Emcee as soon as the performers start to struggle with finding new words from their category.

Pro Tip #1: Try to avoid using the word from the category as the item it would normally describe. For example, if every sentence must include the name of a food, try not to make the scene be about preparing or eating food. Here's a couple of examples of less and more successful choices to follow the rules:

<u>Less successful choices:</u>

'I am hungry so maybe I'll eat an **apple**.'

'Let's go to the **chip** shop and buy **cod** and **chips**.'

As you can see these examples are simply characters talking about food.

<u>More successful choices:</u>

'Darling you are the **apple** of my eye.'

'Come on son, you're a **chip** off the old block'

As you can see these sentences use the food related words as parts of common expressions and will impress your audience more with your word play ability. You could take this a step further and use words in even more non typical ways. For example:

'Where have you **been**?' (as in baked or runner beans)

'We were playing football and **creamed** our opponents.' *(as in fresh or whipped cream)*

'In his **grav-y** was finally at **peas**.' *(In his grave he was finally at peace)*

'And then **Pa-snips** the umbilical cord.'

'In my football kit, cats left a dead mouse.' *(as in Kit Kat)*

SECTION 8: ALL SINGING, ALL DANCING

10 points if you can guess what the games in this section are about from the title...That's right! Geography...or it would be if you were interested in the geography of the West End, or Broadway. Or any place you could dance your happy feet to, with a song in your heart and a tune on your lips!

Nobody puts Baby in the corner...

53: RAP BATTLE

Emcee Intro Script: Next up we are going to have a rap battle. The way this works is two performers will take turns to diss each other through the medium of rap music. At the end you will vote on who you feel won the battle.

Challenge Style: Singing

Players: 2

Ask the audience for:

A relationship between the two players, or two fictional characters who the players could be performing as.

Setup: Ideally, you'll have multiple microphones for this game so the performers can have a microphone each. If you only have one, they will have to swap and share. If you don't have any make sure any backing track of a rap beat isn't too loud so the audience can hear the performers rap over it.

If you have cast members who can beat box to provide a rap beat this can also seem impressive.

How to play the game:

#1: Two players take turns to try to perform a more impressive rap than the other performer.

#2: They can go back and forth taking turns multiple times or have one turn each.

#3: Due to the nature of rap music and 'rap battles' you need to be aware of crossing lines when it comes to bad language, insults and themes. This is something your performers and company can decide upon to meet your own comfort levels and the expectations and standards of your audience.

Pro Tip #1: Identify useful words quickly. If you're doing a rap about the actor Tom Cruise quickly check in with yourself everything you can think of about him that he's well known for – Actor, Mission Impossible, Scientology, Top Gun. That took 5 seconds for me to think of those, and now all I have to do is make sure I mention them in my rap.

Pro Tip #2: Rhyme the important words. It's more satisfying to the audience's ear if you are able to use the words that you have identified as important to the subject as the rhyming words. Below I will give three example rhymes and show how using the important words can enhance the rap.

Example Rap 1:

My name's Tom Cruise and I'm here to rap,

I am a top gun, so shut your trap!

Example Rap 2:

I'm a top gun and my name's Tom Cruise,

So shut your trap, cause I can't lose!

Example Rap 3:

Shut your trap fool and prepare to lose,

I am a top gun and my name's Tom Cruise!

To analyse the three examples, I would say that whilst example 1 is perfectly acceptable, it's also fairly basic. Example 2 and 3 take the route of using the important words 'Tom Cruise' as part of the rhyme. This will be more impressive to an audience who will be amazed that you're able to improvise rhymes that include the words/ideas they've suggested.

Example 3 is even more impressive for the reason that not only have you used the important word as part of the rhyme, but that it also comes as the end of the rhyme.

54: DANCE OFF

Emcee Intro Script: Now we are going to have a Dance Off! Our performers will all dance at the same time and have the opportunity to take the spotlight to show off their best dance moves. The dance moves they will all be doing will be inspired by a profession.

Challenge Style: Dance/Physical

Players: 2-6

Ask the audience for: A profession.

Setup: You'll need enough space for the performers to dance in. Also, you'll need music for them to dance to. This can either be a track played through speakers, or a live performance of music.

How to play the game:

#1: The players all start dancing at the same time, and in true dance off style each takes turns to head to front centre to show off the best moves.

#2: The dance moves should be recognisably inspired by the profession the audience has suggested.

#3: After everyone has danced, the audience are asked to vote on who they felt did the best dance.

#4: If you want to, you could choose two finalists to do a final dance off.

How does the game end?

A Dance Off comes to an end when all the performers have done their dances and the Emcee asks the audience to vote on who they think won.

Pro Tip #1: Try to integrate the most recognisable actions related to the audience suggested profession into your dance. Then mix these in with common dance moves.

For example, if you had to do a dance based on a Fireman you could include moves that resemble climbing ladders, spraying a hose to put out flames and sliding down a pole.

As another example if you had to do a dance based on being a Chef, you could do moves around the idea of chopping vegetables, mixing dough and using a rolling pin.

55: INTERPRETIVE DANCE

Emcee Intro Script: The next game we're going to play is called Interpretive Dance. The performers will create a dance with an inspiration of your choosing.

Challenge Style: Dance/Physical

Players: 1+

Ask the audience for: A recent event that has been in the news, or a well known personality.

Setup: This game is best played with music.

How to play the game:

#1: One player creates a solo dance inspired by the subject matter which the audience have suggested. The dance can be any style, and should give a sense of the story being told and the emotions involved, but should not appear to be an acted scene.

How does the game end? The performer dancing should end the dance themselves after 1-2 minutes.

Pro Tip #1: The game is an interpretive dance, so does not have to be a literal recreation of the subject matter. You can choose to pepper the dance with movements or specific moments that are recognisable to the suggested theme, but should focus more on the quality of movement, and emotions of the dance.

Pro Tip #2: Don't feel the need to purposely do silly dance moves for laughs. If you're a good dancer the audience will enjoy it for that novelty within the context of an improv show. If you're not a strong dancer, try taking it very seriously as if you think you're a dance prodigy, and this will make it funny. Sometimes it can be funnier to watch someone who is bad but thinks they're good than to watch someone bad who acts silly because they know they're bad.

56: KAZOOSICAL

Emcee Intro Script: Our next game is Kazoosical! Our performers will be tasked with creating entirely new pieces of music which they are going to play live for you now...using nothing but kazoos!

Challenge Style: Musical

Players: 1+

Ask the audience for: The name of a piece of music. This could be inspired by a mood.

How to play the game:

Setup: Make sure each player who will be playing this game is provided with a kazoo.

#1: Players create a new piece of music using the kazoos. A kazoo is an instrument that most people should be able to play very easily as it only requires humming into it to play.

#2: If you wish you could make this game more elaborate by having another player make up lyrics to sing a song to the music.

#3: And if you want to be even more elaborate you could bring in additional instruments for more players. I would recommend instruments such as those found in a children's instrument set. This will include things like a miniature xylophone, a triangle, maracas, a tambourine, and even a harmonica.

How does the game end? The players should be able to end their own pieces of music. If you have a player who is reluctant to give up the stage time then the Emcee can end it for them.

Pro Tip #1: Get the players to test their kazoos before the show, as cheap ones can sound terrible.

Pro Tip #2: Also make sure any mouth-based instruments are new or properly cleaned to avoid passing on the dreaded lurgy between players.

Pro Tip #3: Players could also dance to the music being created for extra visual effect. This may be best saved for players who are not playing a kazoo as it may be difficult to play and dance at the same time.

57: SINGING PSYCHIATRIST

Emcee Intro Script: It's time to share your feelings and bare your soul with the Singing Psychiatrist! In this game our performers will take turns to sing about their hang ups, obsessions and fears and get advice sung back to them from the singing psychiatrist.

Challenge Style: Singing

Players: 2+

Ask the audience for:

#1: Fears

#2: Obsessions

#3: An unusual or silly traumatic event

These are assigned to players as the issues that they are visiting the singing psychiatrist to get help with.

Setup: Ideally, you'll have microphones and music to accompany you. Also, if you have chairs or even a couch to sell the idea of it being a therapy session it will add to the presentation.

How to play the game:

#1: Player 1 acts as the singing psychiatrist and welcomes their first patient to tell them about their concerns in life. This intro can either be sung, or spoken as a lead in to the singing.

#2: Player 2 sings about their issues. This includes giving details such as what their issue is, when it started, how it affects their life and so on.

#3: The singing psychiatrist then sings back advice of what Player 2 should do to overcome their issues.

#4: Once the singing psychiatrist has sung the advice, the session is over. If there are more players, it will be the next players turn and the process will repeat.

How does the game end? Once the singing psychiatrist has sung advice to their final patient.

Pro Tip #1: The singing psychiatrist should have a persona that most people would expect from some kind of therapist – caring, listening, knowledgeable, sympathetic etc. Of course, you can always play against these and make the character the opposite for comedic effect.

Pro Tip #2: The rhythm of the game usually goes that the patient sings their problems followed by the psychiatrist singing advice back, but you could always have the exchange go back and forth multiple times, or include bits where you sing together. It's up to you, but I'd suggest if you're considering going for a more complicated structure that you practice it in rehearsals.

58: HOEDOWN

Emcee Intro Script: Next up we're going to have a Hoedown! Our performers will take turns at singing some short funny songs to a catchy tune in this favourite improv classic.

Challenge Style: Singing

Players: 3-5

Ask the audience for: A topic/theme for the songs.

Setup: Hoedown's are often accompanied by a live pianist, and typically feature the very recognisable tune as made famous by the game on the TV show 'Whose Line Is It Anyway?'

There are other tunes that can be used for this game if needed, but if you want to please the improv fans in the crowd then stick to the famous tune.

How to play the game:

#1: The players all stand in a line facing the audience.

#2: They each sing their songs one at a time and follow this basic pattern of 2 verses that have 4 lines each:

Example Hoedown:

I love to sing a hoedown,

It's really really fun!

I sing them in the shower,

And my neighbours start to run!

People hate my singing,

I don't stop take a breath,

But luckily for me,

I can't hear me cause I'm deaf!

#3: After the final player has sung their last line it is traditional for all players to repeat the final line as the music ends.

How does the game end? Once every player has had their turn the game is over.

Pro Tip #1: Players usually try to end on their funniest line. My advice for this would be to quickly think of a fun line that connects to the theme and save that for the ending. As long as the last line is fun, it's not so important if the lines that lead up to it aren't as good.

Pro Tip #2: Practice in your own time. Once you've learned the basic Hoedown tune, it's a really easy game to practice as you're doing other things. The more you practice the better you'll get at making up songs to fit the tune.

59: THREE HEADED BROADWAY STAR

Emcee Intro Script: The next game is Three Headed Broadway Star. In this game 3 performers will create a hit song where they can sing only one word at a time.

Challenge Style: Singing

Players: 3

Ask the audience for: The title of a song that doesn't currently exist.

Setup: As with other singing based games, this is greatly enhanced by having live music or a backing track, but can be played without music.

How to play the game:

#1: The players sing a song where each player can only sing one word at a time.

How does the game end? Once they have finished their song. Often, but not always, you will be able to tell which is the final word of the song and the other players can join in on that word to signify the end.

Pro Tip #1: If you have music in the game, try to make the song you are singing match its style. Faster music will lend itself to more lyrics than slower music would in the same length of time. Slower music will often lend itself to drawing out notes for longer. This said, you can mix this up either way.

Pro Tip #2: As with other games where you can only say one word at a time, really listen to the other performers to make sure the sentences make sense.

Pro Tip #3: Even if you have a great idea, don't try to force it into the lyrics if it doesn't make sense. The other players won't know what your idea is and may take it in a very different direction. This is the nature of the game, and you can't guarantee your idea will make it in as you originally envisioned.

60: LIP SYNC BATTLE

Emcee Intro Script: In this next game you are going to hear incredible singing...because we're going to play famous music and pretend that we're performing it. Get ready for Lip Sync Battle!

Challenge Style: Singing/Dance

Players: 2

Ask the audience for: Song requests. These can either be random or from a limited selection.

Set Up: You will need well known songs for the performers to lip sync to in this game. You could throw the players completely in the deep end by having the audience request songs completely at random, or you could have a limited selection for them to pick from.

Note: You should check into any laws and rules regarding playing well known songs that you do not have the rights to when planning to do this game. If you are playing it at home or at a closed rehearsal you should be able to practice with any songs of your choosing, but if you are considering including this game in a show of any kind you will almost certainly require some kind of licence. The type of licence you need will vary for the venue type, and whether the show is in a theatre/comedy club, broadcast on radio/television or even played virtually over the internet on a live stream or podcast.

How to play the game:

#1: Players take turns to perform their songs.

#2: Players give a full performance of the song, including any dancing and audience interaction they want to, but they do not actually sing the songs themselves. Instead they must lip sync the song to the best of their abilities as if they are the original singer.

How does the game end? The game ends once the songs have been completed. The audience can then vote for their favourite performance. The Emcee can also end a song early if it's a particularly long song and you judge that less is more.

Pro Tip #1: If you don't know the song well just fake it to make it and mime it as best you can and with confidence. The chances are you will be able to get a feel for the song if it has repeating lyrics or you are able to pre-empt how lines may end due to rhymes.

61: GREATEST HITS

Emcee Intro Script: We're now going to have a game of Greatest Hits! In this game our performers are going to introduce you to a great collection of songs, and we'll get to hear a few of them.

Challenge Style: Singing

Players: 2+

Ask the audience for: A subject matter for a collection of music. This could be a type of job like postman, or a type of activity such as horse riding.

Setup: As with other singing based games if you have live music or backing tracks the game will benefit, but if not, it can be played without music. If you have music it would be better to have microphones.

How to play the game:

#1: 1 or 2 players act as hosts of the show and introduce the songs that the singing performers will improvise. Within this introduction they can have banter and give trivia, but their main role here is to make up the name of the song that the singing players will sing.

#2: The singing player(s) improvise the song based on the title they have been given.

How does the game end? It ends after a few songs have been sung.

Pro Tip #1: Try to include a few different styles of songs in the collection. This can be different genres of music, or songs that suggest different emotions. The players acting as the hosts of the show should select a varied range of styles to keep the songs sounding unique from one another.

Pro Tip #2: As you will be performing multiple songs, each song doesn't have to be full length, but more like a highlight clip – 30 seconds to a minute is more than enough.

Pro Tip #3: The songs don't have to rhyme, and you don't need to be the greatest singer to pull this game off. If you can make them rhyme that's great, and if you are a great singer even better. If you are the singing player, and you don't think you can rhyme or are a great singer, just sing your songs confidently and with conviction and you'll do just fine!

62: I'LL SING YOU IN COURT

Emcee Intro Script: In this singing based challenge, players will be assigned the roles of Judge, Defendant, Lawyers and Witnesses and will sing their way through a trial. Also, for extra added fun, you the audience are to play the role of the jury! At the end you will be able to vote on whether the Defendant is found guilty or not guilty!

Challenge Style: Singing/Scene based

Players: 2-5. Assign as many roles as you have enough players for. As a minimum I'd suggest having a Judge and a Defendant. Here is how to assign roles based on your number of players:

2 Players: Judge and Defendant

- Judge sings about the charges and questions the Defendant on the crime. Defendant defends themselves.

3 Players: Judge, Defendant and Prosecution Lawyer

- Judge oversees proceedings, and Prosecution questions the Defendant, who must defend themselves.

4 Players: Judge, Defendant, Prosecution Lawyer and Defence Lawyer

- Judge oversees proceedings, Prosecution and Defence Lawyers each question the Defendant.

5 or more Players: Judge, Defendant, Prosecution Lawyer, Defence Lawyer and Witness characters.

- Judge oversees proceedings, Prosecution and Defence Lawyers each question the Defendant, and any other Witness characters in the game.

Ask the audience for: A unusual crime that the defendant may be accused of.

Setup: This game would be best played with live music as a musician could adapt the length and tone of the music to the timing and mood of the player singing. However, if that isn't possible, a backing track or a cappella are also options. If you have music playing, I would also recommend microphones.

How to play the game:

#1: Each of the players are assigned the roles of Judge, Defendant, Prosecution Lawyer, Defence Lawyer, and Witness depending how many players you have available.

#2: The game begins with the Judge character singing to establish what the Defendant is charged with. End this section asking the defendant how they plead.

#3: The Defendant then takes to the stand and the Defence Lawyer and Prosecution characters take turns at singing their evidence and questions to the Defendant, who will sing back their replies.

#4: If you have enough players you could include them as witnesses for or against the Defendant who come up and sing their views.

How does the game end?

After we have heard from every player, the Judge puts it to the audience (who are treated as the jury) to vote if the Defendant is found guilty or not guilty. You could assign one audience member to be a spokesperson for the jury. Depending if you have a willing participant from the audience you could encourage them to sing either guilty or not guilty after the vote.

Pro Tip #1: This game has a definite structure to follow and may take some rehearsal to get used to the pacing of it. One way to keep order (pun intended) would be to have the performer who plays the Judge either also be the Emcee, or to effectively emcee this game. That way they could call for each performer to take the spotlight at the appropriate time.

Pro Tip #2: Look to conventions of court room scenes and find ways to incorporate them into the format of this game. Objections, side bars, jury deliberations can all be improvised once you know how they would come up in a real court room scene.

SECTION 9: ADAPT AND SURVIVE

Dramatic section title alert! Why is it called 'adapt and survive'? Because all the games within will see you having to quickly adapt your actions and/or words to the actions and words of others. Be very alert, keep on your toes and get ready, or you may not survive the games...although to be honest, you probably will. They're not dangerous.

This is why you should always warm up before doing bullet time...

63: STAND SIT BEND

Emcee Intro Script: In a game of Stand, Sit, Bend, there are three players on stage performing a scene. At all times there must be one player who is standing, one player who is sitting and one player who is bending over. If any player changes the position they are in, the other players must adjust the position they are in to make sure all three positions – stand, sit and bend – are always represented.

Challenge Style: Scene based/Physical

Players: 3

Ask the audience for: A scenario such as a why you may go to battle.

Setup: For best results have one chair centre stage.

How to play the game:

#1: When the game begins the three players should have already assumed the three poses in the scene. One player should be standing up, another player should be sitting down, and another player should be bending over.

#2: Every time one of the players changes the position they are doing, another player has to change what they are doing to ensure that all three positions are represented at all times.

For Example:

Player 1 is standing, Player 2 is sitting on the chair and Player 3 is bending.

Player 1 sits down on the ground resulting in...

Player 1 is sitting, Player 2 is also sitting, and Player 3 is bending.

This means that two players are sitting, and no player is standing. As all three positions must always be represented, Player 2 who was already sitting should change their position to compensate after Player 1 sat down.

This said, Player 3 could have chosen to stop bending and stood up as the standing position had just become free. In this scenario Player 3 would now be standing, but Players 1 and 2 would still be sitting. Player 3 standing here would mean that either Player 1 or Player 2 would need to bend in order for all three positions to be represented as required by the rules.

Pro Tip #1: Whilst you can change between the positions at any point, it is usually more successful if you can justify why you're changing your position within the dialogue and in a way that fits the story you are telling.

If you are changing your position in response to another player changing their position allow them to give their justification as they are leading the changes, and then find a way to justify yours after.

Pro Tip #2: Try to find a balance of how often the positions are changed. If positions are constantly switched the audience will have a hard time following why the changes are being made. On the flip side if there are too few changes of positions the game will lose its appeal.

64: EXTREME STAND SIT BEND

Emcee Intro Script: In a game of Extreme Stand, Sit, Bend we will begin with three players on stage performing a scene. At all times there must be one player who is standing, one player who is sitting and one player who is bending over.

If any player changes the position they are in, the other players must adjust their position to make sure all positions are continually represented.

As this is an extreme version of the game, we will periodically add additional players to the scene with additional positions which likewise must always be represented.

Challenge Style: Scene based/Physical

Players: Minimum of 4

Ask the audience for: A scenario such as a cause for celebration.

Setup: For best results have one chair centre stage.

How to play the game:

The basic rules for the game are the same as a regular game of Stand, Sit, Bend with the following additions:

#1: After about a minute of the scene beginning the Emcee calls 'Freeze'. At this stage they announce that a fourth player will enter the scene with a new starting position such as 'Lie Down'.

The new player would join the scene by laying down and justifying their position with their opening line. The scene then continues under the same rules as before, but now all four positions must be maintained. Any of the players can swap between any other position at any time.

#2: After another 45 seconds of the scene the Emcee will call freeze again, and this time add a fifth player with another new position to be incorporated into the scene.

#3: Then every 30 seconds another new player/position can be added.

How does the game end? By the time there are 5, 6 or 7 players or more the scene will be utter chaos and the audience won't really be able to follow the story anymore. Nor will the players be able to successfully keep track of which positions are or are not being maintained.

The addition of multiple extra players is really just to create chaos, which will be fun to watch for about a minute at most, and that is why I recommend the Emcee adds the final few players in increasingly quick intervals. Once you have all your players on stage jumping about trying to swap positions it is time to end it.

Pro Tip #1: If you are Player 4, or 5 onwards just make a big entrance with your action when entering the scene. There will little opportunity to create a detailed character so just make a splash.

Potential positions to use in this game:

Stand, Sit, Bend, Lie Down, Crouch, Star Jump, Hop, Twerk, Chicken, Tree, Kneel, Pray, Lunge, Downward Dog, Childs Pose, Desperate for the Toilet, Koala, Lean, Slouch, Morris Dance, Power Walk

65: PERSONAL SPACE

Emcee Intro Script: In a game of Personal Space the two performers will create a scene where they must always keep a certain distance away from each other. They will start the scene 6 feet apart, and if one player moves towards the other, the other must move further away to ensure that 6 feet distance has been maintained.

Challenge Style: Scene based

Players: 2

Ask the audience for: Somewhere you wouldn't want to be with someone you didn't like.

Set Up: The two players start the game 6 feet apart.

How to play the game:

#1: The players must always keep at least 6 feet apart. This doesn't mean they can't move further than 6 feet away from each other, but if a player attempts to move closer than 6 feet they must either stop, or the other player will be forced to move away to maintain distancing.

How does the game end? Personal Space ends at the Emcee's discretion. There is an opportunity for the 6 feet rule to be deliberately broken at this stage and the characters to find a cause to come together.

Pro Tip #1: Try to find organic reasons within the story for why it would make sense for the characters to keep away from each other. Don't just move for the sake of it. Here's a few example reasons you could always incorporate into the scene to maintain distance from the other player:

- They smell bad.
- You think they mean you harm.
- There is a magical curse.
- You fancy them and you are worried that you smell bad.
- You are hiding something from them.
- You have stolen something you are keeping secret.
- You're aware that a sniper is planning to shoot them.

- If you touch another human, you will drain their lifeforce.
- You're allergic to their perfume.
- You/they are sick.
- You are trying to get phone signal.
- You don't want to be recognised.

66: EXTREME CHOICES

Emcee Intro Script: The next game is Extreme Choices. In this game, the performers will act out a scene, but every time I call out the phrase 'New choice', the last line that a performer said in the scene will be erased from the script as if they never said it. Then the actor will have to come up with a new choice to replace it. Likewise, I may also call out new physical choice, new emotional choice and a few other ideas that may pop up as well.

Challenge Style: Scene based

Players: 2-4

Ask the audience for:

A scenario which could be inspired from a recent dream they had.

How to play the game:

#1: The players perform a scene, but every so often the Emcee will call out loud one of the following phrases:

New choice
New physical choice
New emotional choice
New accent choice
New spiritual choice
New philosophical choice

Whenever one of these phrases is called out, the player who said the last line before new choice was called out must change their acting choice in the following ways:

New choice: When new choice is called, the last line of dialogue said by a player in the scene has been 'erased from the script' and replaced with a new choice of line of dialogue. These new choices of what to say can be a similar line or can be completely different.

For example:

Player 1: I went to the shop to buy some cheese.

Emcee: New choice!

Player 1: I went to the shop to buy some eggs.

The above would be an example of how you can make a similar new choice to the original choice. Alternatively, you can make a radically different choice. Such as:

Player 1: I went to the shop to buy some cheese.

Emcee: New choice!

Player 1: I sold my boyfriend to the Russian Mafia!

As you can see the new choice this time doesn't relate to the previous idea at all.

New physical choice: If the Emcee calls new physical choice at you, you will need to change your physicality. This can mean going from standing or bending, or walking with a limp, or dancing on the spot. This is a temporary change, so don't feel if your choice is to start jumping that you have to keep jumping continually until told otherwise.

New emotional choice: Change the emotion your character is demonstrating. Once again, don't feel you have to continually do this nonstop. Just do it long enough until a natural opportunity for change occurs.

New accent choice: Change the accent of your character. With this one, you do keep the new accent until instructed otherwise.

New spiritual choice: This is open to interpretation, but should be demonstrated with a greater sense of spirituality (or reduction thereof)

How does the scene end?

The scene ends when the Emcee feels that the scene has reached a natural conclusion or high spot to end on.

Pro Tip #1: You can purposely make your new choices the exact opposite to your original choice for great comic effect. For example:

Player 1: I love your new haircut.

Emcee: New choice!

Player 1: Your new haircut disgusts me.

67: LIE DETECTOR

Emcee Intro Script: Imagine a world where you can't get away with lying. That every time you tell a lie there will be a loud buzzer that reveals you just spoke an untruth. That is the concept for our next game which is called Lie Detector.

In this challenge our performers will create a scene where their characters are not allowed to lie. If they say anything I believe to be a lie, I will press a buzzer and the player who was caught lying will have to explain their lie or tell the truth.

Challenge Style: Scene based

Players: 2+

Ask the audience for: A scenario such as going to a restaurant.

Setup: The Emcee should have a buzzer, or bell to ring whenever they want to challenge a player as lying. Alternatively, they can just call out 'Liar'.

How to play the game:

#1: The players perform a scene, and the Emcee will press the buzzer if they feel anything the characters have said are lies.

The Emcee has full discretion of choosing when they feel a character has lied. This means that a player can say something without intending it to be a lie, but the Emcee can decide it was. This isn't a matter for debate – if the Emcee says it was a lie, then it was a lie.

#2: If the Emcee says something you said was a lie, all characters will be aware you've been caught lying. They can respond to you knowing that you've lied, and it will be up to you to either say the truth or explain your lie.

How does the game end? This game ends when the Emcee feels the scene has played out and reached a satisfactory end point.

Pro Tip #1: As it is up to the Emcee to decide what is or isn't a lie, you could have fun with this by purposely saying things that should be called out as lies such as saying 'the sky is green'. This will give the Emcee the opportunity to not buzz you and if that's the case you've now altered the reality of the world the scene is set in.

Pro Tip #2: Sometimes in real life people lie so they don't hurt each other's feelings. In this game the characters wouldn't be able to do this, so you can have fun with being blunt. For example:

Player 1: Do you like my hair?

Player 2: No, it's hideous.

In real life people probably shouldn't be this blunt, but in this game, you can have as much fun with the characters telling the truth as you can with making them lie.

68: WHOSE LINE

Emcee Note: This game requires the audience to make up lines of dialogue and write them on pieces of paper for the performers to use in the game, so the audience will have to be provided with pens and paper in advance of the game.

Ideally if you provide the audience with these before the start of the show by leaving them at their seats/tables, you can let them know at the start of the show what they will need to do. You can then either get the audience to hand them in themselves or collect them before you play this game in the show. If you have an interval this would be the perfect time to collect the audience lines in.

Emcee Intro Script 1 *(to be said in advance of when you plan to play the game):* So ladies and gents, you may have noticed that next to every seat there is a small square of paper and a pen. Later in the show we will be playing a game where we will be using these, but first we need you to write down a line of dialogue.

By this I mean write down a sentence or two that one person may say to another, like you would find in a film script. Later on, we'll come and collect your pieces of paper to use in the show.

Emcee Intro Script 2: OK our next game is called Whose Line. Now you may remember earlier in the show we asked you all to write down lines of dialogue on small pieces of paper which we collected in during the interval.

In this game our performers will create a scene, and every so often they will read one of the lines you have written as if it is their next line of dialogue.

Challenge Style: Scene based

Players: 2 ideally, but 3 or 4 could work.

Ask the audience for:

#1: Get them to write lines of dialogue on pieces of paper well in advance of the game being played.

#2: A scenario such as a place of work or event that is happening (like a tornado or birthday party).

Setup: You will need to provide the audience with the pens/paper to write lines of dialogue on as explained earlier.

How to play the game:

#1: The performers create a scene and give it enough time to establish the scenario before using any lines.

#2: At regular intervals performers set up the lines written by the audience and sight read them on the spot. Don't read the lines in advance of saying them out loud in the scene.

How does the game end?

This game ends either at the Emcee's discretion or once all audience lines have been used up.

Pro Tip #1: Lines usually work best if you set them up rather than just say them randomly. By this I mean saying something to lead into the audience written line such as:

I remember what my dad told me on my ninth birthday...

When I die I want my tombstone to read...

This reminds me of what it says in the Bible...

Once you have said a set up line like this you will often get a laugh as either the audience line won't make much sense as it will contrast the setup, or it will make sense and the audience will laugh because the line worked! But this brings us to pro tip 2...

Pro Tip #2: Always justify the audience lines!

If you just say a line randomly, there's a good chance the line won't fit your setup line, or even the scene in general. As this is usually the case you should be prepared to follow up the audience line with something to justify why your character has said it. This will help it tie into the scene that you are playing. For example:

If your scene is about a milk factory you could end up saying the following:

Player 1: We're nearly out of milk and the factory is doomed to close...

(Setup line) In times like this I remember what my dad told me on my ninth birthday...

(Audience line) Mountain lions give me panic attacks...

(Justification) You see my dad always had to climb mountains to milk the cows, and if he can do it so can I!

So you can see from this example the player said a set up a line, read the audience line and came up with a line to justify why they said it. This will make the audience line make sense in the scene. Without the justification line, the audience line may still get a laugh as the audience will enjoy their line being read and the randomness of it, but the justification is where you can seal the deal for your big laugh.

Pro Tip #3: Break the fourth wall.

As you are reading out audience lines you do have a bit more freedom to break the fourth wall and acknowledge the audience compared to many other games. You will need to find the balance that works for you and your audience of how much you do this.

You want the audience to be aware when you are reading one of their lines. If you read the lines too discreetly you won't be fulfilling the promise that you made to the audience that you will be reading their lines in the scene. That's what you told them you are going to do, so don't hide it.

Also, when reading audience lines, you can have fun with your delivery. Say it with the passion and emotion that your setup line dictates even if the actual audience line doesn't fit the emotion itself. This contrast will often be funny.

Do they have bad handwriting? Acknowledge that you're struggling to read it. Bad spelling? Likewise have fun with that (but be careful as you don't want to insult your audience). Have they written a monologue? If so, feel free to give up half way and acknowledge that you can't read all that!

Pro Tip #4: You don't have to read out something inappropriate. If the audience have written something that crosses the line, just acknowledge that you're not going to read it and that the audience are naughty. The mystery over what you chose not to read out will probably get a laugh.

69: CONTACT TALK

Emcee Intro Script: Human contact is something we all seek...mostly. In fact some of us try to avoid it. But not in this game! As we are about to play Contact Talk, where our improvisers will perform a scene, but can only speak when they have physical contact with another performer.

Challenge Style: Scene based

Players: 3

Ask the audience for: A scenario such as an activity a group of friends could do together.

How to play the game:

#1: The performers are only allowed to talk when in physical contact with one another. If they are not touching another player, they are not allowed to speak.

How does the game end? The game ends when the Emcee feels the scene has run its course.

Pro Tip #1: Try to find different and creative ways to physically have contact with the other players. A hand on the shoulder is one thing, but will soon become repetitive. Rubbing shoulders, hugs, high fives, shining shoes and Vulcan nerve grips are all alternative ways to make contact.

Pro Tip #2: Respect other player's personal space. An inexperienced player or someone you haven't performed with before may not feel comfortable with people they don't know well having physical contact with them.

They may also not feel comfortable to air these concerns publicly. It would be recommended to say before a show/rehearsal that games such as this may be played and that it's voluntary to take part.

Also make sure players know ground rules for what is acceptable and expected from your company, and that players who are uncomfortable with a game/theme for a scene can withdraw from a game at any time without scrutiny.

70: HEROES AND VILLAINS

Emcee Intro Script: Is it a bird? Is it a plane? No, it's our next game! Which is called Heroes and Villains! In this next scene one of our performers will take on the role of a dastardly Supervillain with an evil scheme to wreak havoc and take over the world. The other performers will play unusual Superheroes who will have to work together to defeat the villain and save the world!

Challenge Style: Scene based

Players: 3+

Ask the audience for:

#1: An unlikely name for a Supervillain for Player 1 and an idea for what their evil plan is.

#2: An unlikely name for a Superhero who will be played by Player 2. Note that you'll only need to ask the audience for one Superhero name, as the performers will decide on additional names during the course of the scene.

How to play the game:

#1: All players in the scene should show off their superpowers which are inspired by the Superhero name they have been given when they enter.

#2: Player 2 is the first to enter the scene and establishes that there is a crisis in the world caused by the Supervillain played by Player 1. The Supervillain will be the last to enter.

#3: Player 2 declares that they cannot save the world on their own and announces the entrance of Player 3 by giving them a Superhero name.

#4: Player 3 enters and also tries to help save the world by using their superpowers.

#5: If there are more players this sequence repeats where the most recent character to enter the scene announces the arrival of the next player. This is always done by endowing the next player with a superhero name.

#6: The only time this changes is when the final player enters the scene who should be Player 1 aka the Supervillain. Player 1 will enter as the Supervillain who is causing the crisis in the world. This will lead to an epic showdown between the villain and the heroes who must use their powers and teamwork to overthrow the villain.

How does the game end? Once the world is safe at the end of the scene.

Pro Tip #1: With an increasing number of players on stage at once, make sure you share the stage and help each other have the best scene possible by putting focus on each other and not hogging the scene for yourself.

Pro Tip #2: You can have fun with the conventions of Superhero movies and comics. You can either choose to play up to typical tropes or subvert them.

SECTION 10: ALL OUT WAR

Improv is all about teamwork and community right? Not in this section! All these games are about outdoing your opponent, reigning victorious, and crushing the skulls of your enemies...figuratively speaking of course...

But speaking seriously for a moment, in case you just read this page and it gives you the wrong impression, improv is always about teamwork even when presented as competitive, so don't get ideas about puncturing your cast mate's tyres or dropping a laxative in their tea at rehearsals!

Remember not to take competitive games too seriously...

71: IMPRESSION BATTLE ROYALE

Emcee Intro Script: We now come to the Impression Battle Royale! Our improvisers are going to do on the spot impressions of historical figures, celebrities and fictional characters. And you will get to vote on who does the best impression. Every player will compete until we have a winner.

Challenge Style: Impressions/Monologue

Players: 2+

Note: This game can either be played in either of the following formats:

2/3 Players: The performers each perform an impression and the audience votes which was best. Whichever player is the first to win three rounds wins the game overall.

4-8 Players: With more players you can play the game as a tournament where players compete in one on one contests and winners advance through to quarter, semi and grand finale rounds. If you have an uneven number of players, you could have rounds contested with three players against each other instead of one on one.

Ask the audience for:

#1: Well know characters from fiction, celebrities or people from history.

#2: Something unusual for the character to be doing.

For example: Harry Potter baking a cake.

Or Henry the Eighth doing karaoke.

How to play the game:

#1: The Emcee will take a suggestion of a character for Player 1 to attempt an impression of, plus an unusual action that you wouldn't expect that character to be doing.

Player 1 then will do their impression. This can last anywhere from 5 seconds to 20 seconds but does not need to be a lengthy monologue. Either the impression will have a clear ending when the actor performing hits a high spot or a big laugh, or the Emcee can interject and end the impression. The Emcee ending the impression can help the player out if they haven't hit upon a big moment so that it doesn't feel like it peters out.

#2: The process is then repeated with Player 2 doing a new impression of a different character.

Note: I wouldn't recommend having both players do an impression of the same character because it would put an unfair advantage to the first player who would be able to use up the most obvious jokes and ideas around the character. On the flip side it would also give Player 2 much more thinking time than Player 1 had if they did the same character. This may seem like the fairness balances things out, but I'd also say having both players doing impressions of two different characters will increase variety in the show.

How does the game end? The audience vote on which impression they preferred. This can be done most effectively by claps/cheers rather than trying to count a show of hands. The player with the most votes wins the round, and if you are playing the game as a tournament they will advance into the next round of the game.

Pro Tip #1: The game is a monologue-based game, so avoid having two players do impressions together as these will become scenes that will take up more time then is needed. Remember, the audience are voting on who does the best/funniest impression, not who can create the best scene.

Pro Tip #2: Contradicting pro tip 1, there are times where a second player can jump in to another player's impression for a quick joke, or if a player is doing an action where a second person on stage would fit the action (such as a character proposing).

I would suggest that these be kept to rare occasions where a great joke can be made, rather than this routinely happen or it will break the concept of the game.

If another player helps you out, did you really win or did the audience vote for the person that helped you?

Pro Tip #3: If you don't know the person you are supposed to be doing an impression of, I would suggest just trying to do it anyway. You can always lean more heavily on the unusual action that the character is doing in these instances.

For example, if you have to do an impression of Supergirl riding a horse, but you don't know who Supergirl is, just do the best darn horse-riding impression that you can!

It will be even funnier if you also just announce that you are Supergirl and use a random choice of accent to make it obvious that while you are doing your best, you also have no idea who the character is.

72: RASSLERS

Emcee Intro Script: Our next game is called Rasslers! Inspired by the over the top world of professional wrestling, our performers are about to go battle...with words! The performers are going to verbally layeth the smack down on each other to reign supreme!

Challenge Style: Monologue/duologue based

Players: 2-4 – Either 1 on 1 or Tag Team 2 vs 2

Ask the audience for:

Unlikely stage names for professional wrestlers. In real life we have wrestlers known as the Undertaker or the Hit Man, but for this game we're looking for something more like The UnderBaker or the Fearless Pony!

Setup: The Emcee can take a more active role in this game by acting as a wrestling style interviewer who is trying to go between the competing improvisers to hype up their match. If they have a microphone this would work well.

How to play the game:

#1: Each performer must state why they are going to defeat their opponent and win an upcoming wrestling match in a stereotypical way that wrestlers speak to hype up matches.

How does the game end? After all the performers have had a chance to talk smack on their opponents the Emcee will ask the audience to vote on who they feel won the war of words.

Pro Tip #1: You should use word play and ideas relating to the wrestler stage name that have been given to you and your opponent.

For example, if your wrestler name is called The UnderBaker you may want to incorporate baking related language such as:

'It must be Easter because I'm **hot**, I'm **cross** and I'm gonna kick you in the **buns**! So, get ready because I'm gonna score the 1, 2, 3 with my **rolling pin**!"

Additionally you would want to use characteristics of your opponent's wrestler name against them. For example:

"You're gonna lose Fearless Pony, because when I'm done with you, you're not gonna feel very **stable**!"

73: DEFINITION BATTLE

Emcee Intro Script: In our next improv challenge our performers will define some made up nonsense words, and you have to decide who created the correct definition.

Challenge Style: Monologue

Players: 2

Ask the audience for: A new word that doesn't already exist.

How to play the game:

#1: Each player takes turns to give the definition of the new word and give examples of how to use it in sentences.

How does the game end? Once both players have given their definitions, the Emcee asks the audience to vote on who they felt gave the correct definition.

Pro Tip #1: It can be fun to treat this game like an academic presentation where you discuss the etymology of the word, its features and usage across the world.

Pro Tip #2: If the opportunity arises it can be fun to use the made-up word later within the same show in a different game. The audience will probably remember the word and will appreciate its use.

74: DEFAMATION BATTLE

Emcee Intro Script: This next game is called Defamation Battle. In it our performers are going to make up scandalous rumours about well know personalities and you have to decide which one is true. That way if we get sued, you were complicit.

Challenge Style: Monologue based

Players: 2

Ask the audience for:

#1: A well-known celebrity, or public figure.

#2: Something else that may be involved in this rumour along with the well-known person. This can be things such as another person, a place, a business, an animal, an object etc etc.

How to play the game:

#1: Each player takes turns at explaining what the rumour they have heard about the well-known public figure is, and how it involves the other element.

How does the game end?

After the performers have both had their turns the Emcee asks the audience to vote which one they most believe to be true.

Pro Tip #1: The more elaborate the stories the better. Don't be afraid to bring in many other elements beyond what the audience suggested to build the story.

Pro Tip #2: If you go second you have the opportunity to play off the fact that the first player's story is incorrect and riff on it to say what actually happened.

75: DEBATE CLUB

Emcee Intro Script: Who doesn't enjoy a good debate? I know I do. So now I'd like to welcome you to our Debate Club. A game in which two performers will argue for and against a hot issue!

Challenge Style: Monologue

Players: 2

Ask the audience for: A topic for which there could be a 'for and against argument'. Try to avoid overly controversial topics, or serious subjects such as real word politics which could split the room.

Set Up: It would be useful to have a stopwatch or timer.

How to play the game:

#1: Each player is given a minute to present their argument either for or against the subject raised.

For example, the topic may be about cloning humans. One player would be against it, and the other would be in favour of it.

How does the game end? Once both players have presented their arguments the audience vote on who they think made the best argument.

Pro Tip #1: It can sometimes feel like you have the more normal, obvious or less controversial argument to make compared to the other player, and that it will be harder to have fun with the subject matter as a result. In these instances, you can lean on making absurd, unexpected or slightly dark arguments which can liven up the perspective.

For example: If you are debating that we should or shouldn't save all the dolphins, I'd expect that most decent people would be in favour of saving dolphins. In this instance it would be easy for the player arguing against saving dolphins to say something outrageous and panto villain like for why dolphins shouldn't be saved. It may then seem more difficult for the player in favour of saving dolphins to make a fun and entertaining argument.

What a player could do here is state that it is short sighted to want to eliminate dolphins considering how intelligent they are. Then argue that the better thing to do would be to genetically enhance them so they can become super dolphins and work for us as underwater spies...or something like that. The point is, there is no reason why the positive argument can't also be dark, absurd and over the top.

Ideas for debate topics

- The Hunger Games should be real.
- The QWERTY alphabet should replace ABC.
- We should all live in virtual reality.
- School is for losers.
- Naked Thursdays.
- Equal rights for ghosts.
- The Purge should be a real thing.
- Electricity should be banned,
- Tickling should be a crime punishable by death.
- Postal workers should be allowed to keep one letter a day.
- Aeroplanes should be designed so their wings flap.

76: ROAST BATTLE

Emcee Intro Script: Get ready to get roasted! Our next game is Roast Battle, and in it our performers are going to act as well-known celebrities, and are going to take turns to roast each other stand up style. One player will be the subject of all of the other player's roasts, but don't worry, they'll get a chance to retort at the end.

Challenge Style: Stand Up Comedy/Monologue

Players: 2+

Ask the audience for: Well-known celebrities or public figures to assign to each player.

How to play the game:

#1: Player 1 is introduced as a well-known person and will be the subject of the other performer's roasts. Player 1 takes a seat to one side of the stage so that their reaction can be seen throughout the scene.

#2: Taking turns, the other players are introduced as additional well-known celebrities who each talk about Player 1's character and make jokes at their expense.

#3: Once all other players have had a turn to roast Player 1, Player 1 is then given an opportunity to roast each of the other players.

How does the game end? After Player 1 has taken their turn to roast all the other players.

Pro Tip #1: Find connections between your character and the character you are roasting. This game gives you two sources to pull references from – your character and character you are making jokes about. For example, if you're playing Mickey Mouse and you're roasting Bill Gates you could draw comparisons that you're both the squeaky voiced faces of evil corporations.

Pro Tip #2: Roasts are based around insult comedy where you make fun of others, so it's important with this game to read the room, and only take things as far as would be acceptable for yourself, your fellow performers, your audience and the standards of your company and venue.

77: CONFESSION KOMBAT

Emcee Intro Script: Generally speaking, our performers are very bad people...we just hide it better than most of you in the audience. But not anymore! In our next game, which is called Confession Kombat, our performers will take the blame for unusual crimes and confess why they have done the unthinkable.

Challenge Style: Scene based

Players: 2+

Ask the audience for: A crime or something else you may have done that you would feel guilty about.

How to play the game:

#1: The flow of this game is that Player 1 will start by confessing to the audience that they have committed the crime that the audience suggested. They will then proceed to explain why they did it.

#2: At this point, Player 2 will step forward and denounce the first player saying that Player 1 was covering for them. They will then explain 'the truth' about how it was actually them that committed the crime and why they did it.

#3: At this stage Player 1 takes over again to reclaim guilt and create an even more elaborate version of the truth.

This pattern can continue for as many times as the players want until the scene ends.

How does the game end? The Emcee will stop the players squabbling over who is going to take the blame, and can then ask the audience who they believe is the true guilty person.

Pro Tip #1: Build upon the stories already told. The more versions of the story the players say, the more content they will have to draw upon to create the next version of the confession.

For example, if Player 1 said they did the crime and it involved a wolf stealing a car, Player 2's version of the story could also involve a wolf, but it could be that they confess they are a werewolf to put a different spin onto its involvement.

78: BAKE OFF

Emcee Intro Script: For our next game we're going to play Bake Off! Competing players will use real food to create delicious designs based on your suggestions!

At the end you can vote on who you think made the best design and you can actually eat the results...if you have a death wish. Disclaimer: We take no responsibility if an audience member eats one of our improviser's Bake Off creations and becomes ill including, but not limited to cooties, the dreaded lurgy and the Ebola virus. OK let's get on with the game!

Challenge Style: Cooking

Players: 2-4

Ask the audience for: An artistic design to create using food. This can be based on things such as geographical locations, well known stories, or people.

Setup: For this game you will need to provide your performers with lots of food items and ingredients to create their deigns with. If possible the food preparation should take place on a table and you should ensure that you have sheets on the tables and possibly on the stage itself to prevent mess that will interfere with the rest of your show.

Note: If you plan to play this game it is worth avoiding using nuts, and checking with any participants if they have any allergies that could pose a risk. Check food packaging for allergy information, but also ask players if there's anything you should be aware of when planning this game.

How to play the game:

#1: The players have to create artistic designs that represent the audience suggestion using the available food items.

#2: The players are given a 3-minute time limit to complete their task.

#3: During the game, the Emcee can act as host of the Bake Off and interview the participants in ways typically found in reality TV cooking shows.

How does the game end? Once the time limit has passed the Emcee will ask the players to show off and explain their creations. The audience can then vote on who they feel did the best.

Pro Tip #1: Even with a time limit of just 3 minutes, this can feel a long time for the audience if the performers are concentrating too much on making their food creations. Don't forget that you can still be in character and play off the tropes of TV cooking shows to win over the audience with your characterisation.

Pro Tip #2: When it comes to making the artistic design with the food, keep in mind the size of the audience and that people sat at the back may not be able to see your work as clearly as the front row. Keep your designs big and bold as this may be a rare instance where quantity wins out over quality if the audience simply can't see small details.

79: RAISE THE STAKES

Emcee Intro Script: Our next improv challenge is called Raise the Stakes! And in this game the players are going to start a scene with a fairly ordinary scenario but have the goal of continually raising the stakes as the scene goes on.

Challenge Style: Scene based

Players: 2+

Ask the audience for: A mundane situation.

How to play the game:

#1: Players start creating an ordinary scene.

#2: The more the scene progresses, the higher the performers should raise the stakes within the story. This can be through events that happen within the scene, revelations of secrets, actions, dialogue and performance styles.

How does the scene end? The Emcee should call an end to the scene when they feel that the stakes cannot be raised any more, or that the scene reaches a natural conclusion.

Pro Tip #1: The performers should raise the stakes of the scene in stages and not all in one go. If you raise them too high too fast you won't have anywhere else to take the scene.

For example don't go from 'I've spilt the milk' directly to 'You spilt the milk on the nuclear detonator now we have 3 seconds to live!' as it would be difficult to continue raising the stakes from here.

Pro Tip #2: Be careful that the scene doesn't just become very shouty. The scene lends itself to panic, heightened emotions/acting and arguments between characters, but it doesn't always have to be this way.

The goal isn't just to one up the other player in a competitive way. The game can also be played as a team and work together to create a situation which gets increasingly more desperate.

80: COMPULSIVE LIARS

Emcee Intro Script: Our next game is Compulsive Liars. In this scene everything our performers say must be a lie. If they're caught telling the truth they lose a life. If they lose a life, they lose a limb! When a player loses all their lives, it's game over and the other player wins! We'll occasionally allow a question to slip through the cracks, as generally questions can't be either true or false, but over use of questions will also result in a lost life!

Challenge Style: Scene based

Players: 2

Ask the audience for: A scenario such as a suggestion of some kind of reunion.

How to play the game:

#1: As you perform the scene you have to ensure every line you say is a lie.

#2: The only exception to this rule is that you are allowed to ask questions, and generally speaking questions can't be lies. For example, if you asked 'How are you?' this sentence cannot be interpreted as lie, but may be required to continue the scene.

Questions of this nature should only be used sparingly to keep the flow of the scene going, and the Emcee can penalise you for overuse of questions.

It is possible for a question to be a lie if it includes untrue information. For example:

Player 1: Why did you kill me?

Unless you're in a scene about a ghost, quite clearly Player 1 is lying here as a dead person can't ask why you killed them. A less clear-cut example would be:

Player 1: Why did you poison my drink?

This question from Player 1 assumes that Player 2 poisoned their drink, which for the purpose of this example we'll say they categorically did not do. This doesn't guarantee that this question was intended as a lie, but as more of an accusation. In this instance it would be at the Emcee's discretion to take the question as a lie or not.

How does the game end? This game ends when a player has lost all of their lives.

Pro Tip #1: Try to make the lies you say relate to the scene, and not just be random sentences. So, if you're in a scene about being stuck in quicksand you could say 'I'm not worried' when clearly your character is and should be worried. Saying random sentences such as 'Gorillas have eight legs' is a lie but doesn't relate to what's happening in the scene. It may be fun to throw a few things like this in but shouldn't be the focus of what you say.

SECTION 11: WHO GOES THERE?

This section is all about guessing games. To have fun with this idea, can you, the reader, guess what is the thing that the title of this section references? You can find out the answer in the Afterword at the end of this book...

Who will have the last laugh?

81: MYSTERY MURDER

Emcee Intro Script: We're now going to play the game Mystery Murder. We're going to ask one of our performers to leave the room, and whilst they're away we're going to decide several details of a crime they have committed. When they come back, they will answer questions from our other performers about the crime, as they try to figure out what the crime they have committed is.

Challenge Style: Guessing game

Players: 2+

Setup:

The performer playing the murderer needs to leave the room whilst suggestions are taken from the audience. This is to ensure that the player cannot hear the suggestions. If this isn't possible, the 'murderer' could wear headphones with music playing to prevent them hearing the audience suggestions.

Ask the audience for:

#1: A well-known character from fiction or history who is the murder victim.

#2: A second well-known character from fiction or history that the performer who left the room will be playing.

#3: A motive for why they killed their victim.

#4: A method/weapon that was used to commit the crime.

How to play the game:

#1: The murderer has to answer questions from the other players with confidence as if they know who they are playing and what they are being asked about.

#2: The other players should ask questions that hint to, but do not give away the details of the murder. The longer the game goes the more obvious the clues should become.

For example, if the murder victim was Fred Flintstone you shouldn't ask 'Why did you kill Fred Flintstone?' as that gives away one of the things the murderer is trying to guess.

Instead you should ask questions that give clues to the details they need to guess. So, if the victim was Fred Flintstone these may be some questions that will help the murderer guess the identity of their victim without you directly saying it to them:

"I heard you and the victim were arguing all the time, and on the day of the murder got into a bit of a **barney**. Is this true?"

"Did you hear the victim's wife was distraught? Her life has been turned to **rubble**. Well worse than that. Just little **stones** and **pebbles**."

"We know you killed him. But tell us, why did you **dabba do** it?"

The words highlighted in bold show clue words that relate to the Flintstones theme. A player shouldn't make these words stick out like a sore thumb, but they also shouldn't say them so subtly that they cannot be picked up on as clues.

How does the game end? The game ends when the murderer has clearly worked out who they are, or the Emcee judges that enough time has passed, and they may not have figured it out yet.

Either way, the Emcee should directly ask the murderer who they are playing, who they have killed, why they killed them and by what method? If they guess correctly you should encourage the audience to clap.

If they guess incorrectly you can give the player huge clues as a last ditch effort for them to win the game. If they still can't figure it out...just tell them.

Pro Tip #1: If you're playing the murderer remember that you are always in character. This means you should speak as if you are the character, and not talk about the murderer as a third person.

Additionally, as you are playing a character who is a murderer you can have fun with the idea of whether you want to admit that you are guilty or not. You could play it as if you deny the charges, or you could proudly proclaim that you are the guilty person.

Pro Tip #2: If you are playing the murderer and you think you have worked out one of the things you need to guess, I would suggest that you don't say something like 'I guess I killed Fred Flintstone' as that breaks character.

Instead you could stay in character and say something that reveals that you have figured it out. For example, you could say "I didn't do it. I've never even been to **Bedrock**, and don't know who this Flintstone person you're all talking about is."

If you're right in figuring out that you killed Fred Flintstone, the audience will laugh/clap and respond positively to what you have said.

If it turns out you've made a mistake and you thought you killed Fred Flintstone, but this is the wrong character I would suggest that the Emcee help you out by indicating that this isn't correct. You can brush this off in character by hinting that you were thinking of another murder you had committed.

82: PARTY QUIRKS

Emcee Intro Script: The next game we are going to play is Party Quirks! One of our performers is going to play the host of a party and the others will play the guests. Each of the guests will arrive one at a time, and they will each have a strange 'quirk' that our host will have to figure out.

Challenge Style: Scene based/Guessing game

Players: 4+

Ask the audience for: Quirks for each party guest. Examples could be:

- Thinks they're a dog.
- Has time travelled here from the future.
- Bursts into song when nervous

Note: This game can be played by asking the audience to suggest the quirks for each guest, but the performer playing the host of the party would need to step out the room or wear headphones so they can't hear the audience suggestions.

Otherwise the performers can have quirks that have been assigned to them secretly, but this game works better if the audience have an awareness of the quirk that the party host is trying to guess.

How to play the game:

#1: The performer who is playing the party host starts in the scene alone to get ready for their party.

#2: After about 20 seconds the first guest arrives and interacts with the party host as if they know each other. The host should play along as if they know who their guest is. They can offer them drinks, food and make general chit chat.

#3: The performer playing the guest should say and do things that will give hints about what their quirk is without directly giving it away.

#4: When the host feels they have a sense of who the guest is they should say their guess whilst still remaining in character and not breaking the fourth wall to make their guess.

For example, if the guest was 'Someone addicted to Pepsi' the host could say their guess like this:

'Hope you're enjoying the party. I made sure we only have water tonight as I didn't want to send you off the wagon with the fizzy brown stuff...'

This line would make it obvious that the party host has worked out what the guest's quirk is. This would be a better choice than the following where the performer breaks character to guess.

'I think I know what their quirk is. Is she addicted to Pepsi?'.

#5: Each guest should enter after about minute long intervals. It doesn't matter if the host hasn't guessed the previous player's quirk already. Just like in a real party the host may have to juggle their attention to entertain all their guests.

How does the game end? The game ends once the host has guessed the quirks of all the guests. If it appears they won't be able to correctly guess all the quirks the Emcee can help out or end the game by saying what the quirks were.

Pro Tip #1: If you are a party guest with a quirk don't make it too obvious what your quirk is. Play the character, but don't give it away instantly by saying your name/quirk or by giving too obvious a clue.

Be selective in the clues you give and make it progressively more obvious as the game goes on. For the purposes of the show we want the party host to be able to guess who you are, but we also don't want the scene to be over instantly because you made it too obvious.

Pro Tip #2: If you are a party guest and the party host is interacting with another guest don't pull focus away from them by doing something loud or by starting another conversation in the scene.

It's important to stay in character even if you're not the focus of the scene, but don't make the mistake of starting a second scene within the one already in progress! This will only serve to divide the audience's attention. Pick your moments and if all performers practice good stage craft and share the stage time, everyone will get equal opportunities to be in focus.

This quirky party guest is a scream!

83: CHARODEO

Emcee Intro Script: Our next game is called Charodeo and is a high energy and competitive version of charades! Two players will perform two separate mimes based on films/books/songs etc...at the exact same time.

As they are doing this, the audience will have to shout out and guess what they think the performers are trying to mime. Whichever player is able to give the best clues to have their mime guessed first defeats their opponent. Also, whichever audience member is able to guess correctly first is also a winner!

Challenge Style: Guessing game/Physical

Players: 2

Ask the audience for: Nothing in this game as it is the audience who must guess what the players are performing.

Setup: The Emcee should whisper to each player what they will be miming so that the audience cannot hear.

How to play the game:

#1: The competing players occupy one side of the stage each as their performance zone. They will both be performing at the same time, so it's important that both players allow the other a fair amount of space.

#2: When the game begins the players have to mime things to which could be clues to the words of the name of the film/book title.

Alternatively, they can choose to mime clues that directly relate to the content of the film/book.

For example, if a player has to give clues to the film 'Terminator 2: Judgement Day' they could mime that they are a judge and bang a gavel to give the audience a clue to the word judgement. This clue would be to the word and not actually relate to the content of the film they are giving clues to.

For a different approach, the player could crouch down on one knee and slowly rise up like Arnold Schwarzenegger famously does in every Terminator film. This clue doesn't hint at the definition of any of the words in the film's title but instead relies on the audience having direct knowledge of the content of the film.

#3: As the performers are acting in mime, the Emcee can provide commentary and encourage the audience to call out guesses as soon as they have an idea of what either performer is miming.

#4: The players miming are not allowed to speak or make vocal noises. They are not allowed to mime words that can be lip read.

#5: They are also not allowed to write words down or point to words or letters to give clues to a film's title. There may be exceptions to this last point. For example, if a player is tasked with miming something like Agatha Christie's book 'The ABC Murders', may be forgiven for indicating letters of the alphabet at the Emcee's discretion.

How does the game end? It ends as soon as an audience member calls out a correct guess of one of the players' mimes. At this point the Emcee can congratulate the audience member for winning the game. The Emcee can also congratulate the performer whose mime they were able to guess as they were able to more successfully do their mime compared to their opponent.

The Emcee should then also reveal what the losing player's mime was. If a correct guess comes very quickly into the game, the Emcee can make the judgement call to allow the losing player to continue their mime to extend the length of the round.

Pro Tip #1: This game is not exactly the same as playing charades. Cut out the parts where you mime first word/second word, sounds like and number of syllables.

This is an acting based game, so you should concentrate on giving performance based clues. Remember you're in a race against your opponent who will also be performing clues, so by the time you have established it's a book with four words, and the first word has three syllables, and the first syllable sounds like...they may have already won the game.

Pro Tip #2: Repetition is your friend! Remember that both you and your opponent will be miming at the exact same time. It's very possible that audience members may miss a vital clue you are doing in your mime if they are watching the other player. With this in mind, make sure you lean towards big bold actions as clues, and do them several times over so that everyone in the audience has had a chance to see them!

SECTION 12: WHAT'S IN A TITLE?

The games in this section all limit the way you can communicate to just saying the titles from particular categories.

84: SONG TITLES

Emcee Intro Script: Now we're going to play Song Titles. In this game our performers are only allowed to speak in song titles.

Challenge Style: Scene based

Players: 2-4

Ask the audience for: A scenario such as a place where people meet.

How to play the game:

Setup: 2 players perform at a time and when a player is eliminated another player swaps with them. Nonperforming players should wait on a backline or at the side of the stage ready to enter.

#1: Players are only allowed to say the names of famous songs as their way of communication. No other words are allowed to be used in the sentences.

#2: Generally speaking, you shouldn't try to string several song titles together to form larger sentences. The song title on its own should always be recognisable to the audience, and combining several song titles together will require the audience to have to decipher where one title ends and where the next begins.

#3: If a player says something that isn't a song title they are eliminated and have to swap with a player who isn't in the scene. This player will join as a new character and not as a continuation of the previous player's character.

#4: If a player hesitates for too long, they are eliminated from the game and have to swap with another player.

How does the game end? At the Emcee's discretion.

Pro Tip #1: To get better at this game do some research on well-known song titles. The audience will enjoy hearing you use a song title they know, so popular songs are best to use in this regard.

Pro Tip #2: If you can use song titles that relate to the scenario all the better! For example, if your scenario was about aliens and you use song titles such as

Space Man, Fly me to the Moon and Life on Mars these would all relate to the theme of space and aliens.

Pro Tip #3: You can get away with some poor choices for comedic effect. So, if your scenario was space aliens and you simply said 'Star Wars Theme' it wouldn't seem the best title to say to further your scene, but the audience would understand the connection.

85: MOVIE TITLES

Brief description of the game: Movie titles works exactly the same as the game Song Titles, but instead of speaking only in song titles, you can only say the names of well-known movies in order to communicate.

Pro Tip #1: Unlike songs, movies frequently have sequels which can be used in this game as come backs to what has already been said. For example:

Player 1: Look Who's Talking!

Player 2: Look Who's Talking Too!

Pro Tip #2: Movies also often have subtitles, and if these are recognisable enough on their own, they could be used separately and not as part of the full title of the film. For example, you could just say 'A New Hope' and not have to say 'Star Wars: Episode 4: A New Hope'.

This said, saying the full title may be funny if you can emphasise that the only reason you are saying the full title is to use the 'A New Hope' part. The subtitle here would still further your scene, and the rest of the title would add to the comic effect.

86: BOOK TITLES

Brief description of the game: As you can probably guess, Book Titles is another version of Song or Movie Titles, but this time you can only communicate by saying the names of books.

Pro Tip #1: Book titles can have a lot of cross over with movie or song titles, but there are also many types of book titles that you would never find in the other categories. This may include self help books, religious texts, autobiographies, history books, diaries and even shopping catalogues.

SECTION 13: BOW TIE BREAKER GAMES ARE COOL

Sometimes a competitive game will end in a draw, or without a clear winner. These games will give you a quick way of deciding a winner.

No ties were broken in the making of this book.

87: CATEGORY BATTLE

Emcee Intro Script: OK so sometimes we need a tie breaker to settle a competitive game when it is too close to call or we have a draw. A Category Battle isn't really a game that requires acting skills, but it does require quick thinking and fast reactions. Our two performers will take turns to name items from a category in quick succession without hesitation, without repeating something that has already been said and without saying something that doesn't belong in the category. The first to break one of these rules loses and the other will stand victorious!

Challenge Style: Tie Breaker

Players: 2

Ask the audience for: A category

How to play the game:

#1: Players take turns to name things that belong in the suggested category.

#2: If a player repeats something that has already been said they lose.

#3: The Emcee should give the players a maximum of 3 seconds to say their next answer. If the player doesn't give an answer this quickly, they lose.

#4: If the player says something that doesn't belong in the category they lose.

How does the game end? The game ends when one of the players breaks a rule.

Pro Tip #1: The Emcee should be selective of what they accept as a category from the audience. If for example they suggest 'food' or 'animals' you may find the category is too broad and that the game wouldn't end quickly as there are too many potential answers. Instead ask the audience to narrow things down to a specific type of food or a type of animal such as mammals or reptiles.

Example good categories:

Fruits, Vegetables, Disney princesses, US States, Types of cars, Marvel characters, Breeds of dog, Films starring Keanu Reeves, Countries in Europe, Chocolate bars, Elements, Mythological creatures

Example bad categories:

Foods, Actors, Years, Smells, License plate numbers, Songs, Crimes you have committed, Things my uncle bought yesterday, Girls names, Letters of the Alphabet, Methods of picking things up, Words in a dictionary

88: THE ROCK, NEWSPAPER, TERMINATOR

Emcee Intro Script: We need to play a tie breaker game here, and whilst we could play something as simple as Rock, Paper, Scissors, we're going to take that concept to the next level! As we are going to play The Rock, Newspaper, Terminator!

I'll be honest, this game works exactly like Rock, Paper, Scissors...it just sounds more exciting this way.

Just as Rock beats Scissors we believe that Dwayne The Rock Johnson is the only human in the world tough enough to beat Arnold Schwarzenegger's Terminator. But just as Paper beats Rock, a scandal in a newspaper is enough to bring The Rock smacked down to his knees. And as Scissors is able to defeat Paper, not even a scandal in a tabloid newspaper can affect a machine...so Terminator beats Newspaper.

Challenge Style: Tie Breaker

Players: 2

Ask the audience for: N/A

How to play the game:

#1: The Emcee can oversee the game by counting the players in with a 3, 2, 1...shoot!

#2: On 'Shoot' the players both must perform a pose that represents either The Rock, A Newspaper or The Terminator. Here are our suggestions of how each should be done:

- The Rock: Cross both arms back and forth in front of your stomach with your index finger pointing on each hand. This is a signature pose the Rock would do whilst setting up for the People's Elbow wrestling move.
- Newspaper: Place your hand together out in front of yourself and open them as if they are a book (or in this case, a newspaper).
- Terminator: Put both hands out in front of yourself as if the fingers are pistols.

#3: The way you win works as follows:

The Rock defeats Terminator

Terminator defeats Newspaper

Newspaper defeats The Rock

If there is a tie you go again until there is a winner.

Pro Tip #1: It's Rock, Paper, Scissors...

Pro Tip #2: If this elaborate version doesn't work for you, you can replace Rock, Paper or Scissors with any other words and poses you wish...or you know...you could just play Rock, Paper, Scissors as nature intended.

89: FIND IT!

Emcee Intro Script: We need to play a tie breaker game. Here is a quick challenge. Our performers have 30 seconds to find something from their environment that represents an emotion of your choice. Once they have found it, I will decide who the winner is.

Challenge Style: Tie Breaker

Players: 2

Ask the audience for: An emotion.

How to play the game:

#1: The performers will get 30 seconds to complete the task.

#2: The performers have to find something from their environment that best represents an emotion. To complete this task, they can find an object or combination of objects from the performance space, an audience member, the dressing room or anywhere else nearby. They can go wherever they like as long as they are ready to present their efforts at the end of 30 seconds.

Example:

If players are tasked with finding something that represents happiness here are some options of what they could present:

- A chocolate bar they have borrowed form an audience member.
- A pile of leaflets which have been scrunched up to resemble a heart.
- A hug given to the Emcee.

How does the game end? The Emcee will decide who has given the better effort of the players. This game is useful when another competitive game doesn't have a clear winner from its rules, or an audience vote is split. The Emcee's decision is final.

Pro Tip #1: Don't get too into this challenge and insist that an audience member helps you. Look for willing participants, but if they're not keen don't push people to be involved. They might be on the side of your opponent, or just not want to play along.

SECTION 14: STORY TIME

The focus of the games in this section is all about telling stories. Yes, arguably almost all of the games in this book are about creating and telling stories, but these ones in particular are about story telling.

You will burst with excitement to play these games!

90: ONE WORD STORY

Emcee Intro Script: Next up we're going to tell you a story! Our performers will stand in a line and make up a story where each player can speak one word at a time.

Challenge Style: Story telling

Players: 2+

Ask the audience for: The name of story, and/or characters the story is about.

Setup: The players all stand in a line facing the audience.

How to play the game:

#1: The players can each only say one word at a time.

#2: The players usually speak in the order from stage right to stage left, and this order repeats throughout the entire game.

How does the game end? Hopefully the players can get a sense of how long the story has been going and can begin to wrap it up naturally themselves. If this isn't happening the Emcee can step in and end it for the team.

Pro Tip #1: Don't announce punctuation such as full stops. There are some people who do play the game this way, but I would recommend not to, because it isn't the usual way for people to speak and comes across jarring. An audience should be able to understand when a sentence has come to a natural end from the tone of your voice and the words said.

Pro Tip #2: Do allow sentences to end! A common mistake people make when playing this game is using words such as 'and', 'but' and 'because' over and over again. This adds clauses to sentences and doesn't allow the sentences to end.

Pro Tip #3: Avoid using the word 'I' unless the story is quoting a character's dialogue. As you are telling the story as a group it can become confusing for the audience if you tell the story from a first person perspective. Say for example the subject of the story was Harry Potter and as a team you said the following sentence:

'One day Harry was in the library and **I** saw him eat a frog.'

The audience would understand who Harry is, but you have now cast yourself as a mystery character in the story. This will confuse the audience as it won't be clear if the 'I' refers to the performer who said it, or if all the players represent the same person.

Also due to the nature of the game, it's quite unlikely you'll all be on the same page enough to resolve that your story now features a mystery unknown protagonist who the story is being told from the perspective of.

Pro Tip #4: Don't forget what the story is about! It can be very easy with this game for you to get side-tracked away from the subject that the audience suggested you make up the story about. Some players may start a game and take a long time to even reference what the story was supposed to be about. To avoid this, just keep in mind what the promise was to the audience and look for opportunities to include related material in the story.

It can be frustrating if you want to reference the audience suggestion, but don't get the opportunity to incorporate relevant words on your turn. Sometimes you'll have no choice but to say connective words such as 'the' or 'in' just to keep the sentences making sense. Unfortunately that can be the luck of the draw in this game. Stay calm, be patient and when the opportunity comes up to include bigger words take it!

Pro Tip #5: Always keep the story going forwards! Mistakes will happen. Someone will mishear someone else, repeat a word or say something that doesn't make sense grammatically. If this happens and you can't think how to make the sentence make sense, just pause for a moment and start a new sentence. By using your tone of voice, you can indicate that this is a new sentence and not a continuation of the last one.

Additionally, if you think a sentence has gone south and isn't working, you can bet that the audience may be thinking the same thing. A brief expression of confusion on your face before continuing can go a long way to communicating to the audience that you are as aware as they are that something went wrong. This will help keep them on side with your team to keep going.

91: STORY STORY DIE

Emcee Intro Script: Our next game is called Story Story Die. All our performers will stand in a line and I will point at one player at a time. Whoever I point to must continue telling the story until I stop pointing at them. As soon as I stop pointing at them, they have to stop telling the story even if they are in the middle of a sentence or the middle of a word.

Whenever I point to a different player that player must continue telling the story from exactly where the previous player left off. This includes finishing off the sentence or word.

If they fail to continue telling the story from exactly where the last player stopped speaking or if they hesitate by saying things like 'errr' or 'ummm' they are eliminated from the game. We will continue this game until there is only one player left who will be our winner.

The audience can help judge this one. If you notice anyone break the rules, I want you shout 'Die' at that player. Let's give it a practice. 1, 2, 3...Die!

Challenge Style: Story Telling/Elimination

Players: 4+

Ask the audience for: A main character of the story and a household object.

Setup: The players all stand in a line facing the audience whilst the Emcee stands or kneels a few feet in front of them so they can point to individual cast members.

How to play the game:

#1: Players have to continuously tell the story for as long as the Emcee is pointing at them.

#2: If the Emcee points away from you whilst you are speaking you must stop immediately. If you continue speaking after the Emcee has pointed away from you, you are eliminated from the game.

#3: If the Emcee points to you, you must pick up the story from exactly where it left off and continue it from there. If a word or sentence has gone unfinished you must finish it, or you will be eliminated from the game.

#4: The audience should be encouraged to be the judge of the game. If they don't shout die and are being too nice to the performers, the Emcee can step in and call die when a player goes wrong.

The Emcee may come across like the bad guy here, but if this game isn't strictly judged it can go on forever.

#5: Once a player has been eliminated the Emcee should get the audience to clap the eliminated player and start the game again with just the remaining players stood in line on stage.

How does the game end? This game ends when there is only one player left standing and is therefore the winner.

Pro Tip #1: The Emcee can vary the order in which they point to the performers, and how long they point to each player. This does give the Emcee a certain level of power to play unfair towards players, but hopefully if you're the Emcee, you'll play it fairly...or do it unfairly in the interest of comedy. It is just a game after all.

Pro Tip #2: If you are a player in the game always look at the Emcee rather than looking at another player who may be telling the story. If you are watching the other players you are likely to miss when the Emcee points to you, and you will be eliminated.

Pro Tip #3: Don't backtrack. If the player speaking before you says 'Rachel was going to the...' you shouldn't repeat any of their words such as saying 'Going to the shop to cuddle puppies.' To do so would make the overall story 'Rachel was going to the going to the shop to cuddle puppies.' And that doesn't make any sense.

Pro Tip #4: If you didn't hear what the previous player was saying...too bad. Don't give excuses for why you feel you shouldn't be eliminated from the game, cause that ain't gonna fly in prime time! Unless it's done very jokingly the audience will turn on you.

92: SCARY STORY

Emcee Intro Script: Audience beware, you're in for a scare...because we're about to tell you a Scary Story...

Challenge Style: Story telling/Monologue

Players: 1+

Ask the audience for: The title of the scary story.

How to play the game:

Setup: This would be a good game to have the lights dimmed for, and if possible, have some quiet atmospheric music in the background. If you have a smoke machine available let her rip!

#1: The performing player tells an atmospheric story which can mix both horror and thriller elements with comedic elements.

#2: Generally speaking, this is a one player game, but multiple players could tag in and out to continue telling the story. This would be done by a player tapping the storyteller on the shoulder to indicate that they wish to take over.

#3: Players who aren't telling the story can get involved in other limited ways by acting out things in mime or by vocalising sound effects.

Note: If you are supporting the storyteller in this way, just be careful not to pull focus away from the story they are telling.

How does the game end? Players should be able to end their own stories, and the Emcee should only intervene if the scene has gone on noticeably too long.

Pro Tip #1: Use contrast to great effect. Try drawing the audience in with a quiet and calm voice and little or slow movement before bursting to life with screams, running around and big movements in your scary story.

Pro Tip #2: Judge your audience carefully. Even though this game is called Scary Story, you still have to be mindful that the focus of most games in this book are comedy games.

If you play this game too seriously or tell a truly disturbing story it may be jarring or upsetting to an unprepared audience who just wanted to see some actors doing silly word games. It may be that a genuinely spooky story will be a nice change of pace and variety in the show, but it is up to you how far you wish to push things in a darker direction.

93: POEM OF THE WEEK

Emcee Intro Script: Up next, we are going to give you a poetry recital like you've never heard before! This is our poem of the week.

Challenge Style: Monologue/Poetry

Players: 1+

Ask the audience for: A subject matter for the poem.

How to play the game:

#1: The performing player improvises a poem based around the theme suggested by the audience.

How does the game end? The poem should be ended by the player performing it.

Pro Tip #1: There are many different styles of poems, and in this game you have the freedom to draw on any of these styles to create your poem.

Will it rhyme or not? If it does rhyme what rhyming pattern will you use? AABB? ABAB? Etc?

Are you going to stand still as you deliver it, or will it be more of a performance that uses the entire stage?

These are questions you can decide the answers for yourself, so the biggest tip here is to read, watch and listen to other poets to get some ideas of how you could approach performing one yourself.

94: ONE MINUTE LEFT TO LIVE

Emcee Intro Script: The next game is called One Minute Left to Live, and will see one of our performers living their last minute.

Challenge Style: Solo Scene

Players: 1

Ask the audience for: A well-known character from fiction, and an unusual way for them to meet their demise.

Setup: You will need a stopwatch or timer to time the one minute.

How to play the game:

#1: The performer performs the final minute of the life of the character they are playing before acting out an elaborate and dramatic stage death.

How does the game end? Death ends this game. Either that or the Emcee can end it, if the performer doesn't die within the allocated minute. I would recommend comically shooting them to put the character out of their misery.

Pro Tip #1: Before you get to the death for the character, you can play around with what the character is doing in the minute leading up to their untimely end. Are they aware they are about to die? If so, how do they respond? They may be brave, they may panic, or they may want to live out one last dream to tick off the bucket list.

Pro Tip #2: With regard to the way the character dies, the more melodramatic and slapstick it is the better. You could also play with contrast and expectations such as giving a character like Elmo a Shakespearian-like final monologue before they die. Or by giving a stereotypically brave character such as Neo a tear filled hissy fit as he meets his doom.

A dramatic end to a dramatic scene...

95: ONE PERSON FIGHT CLUB

Note: This game centres around a performer creating a one-person fight scene, and can therefore include improvised stage combat. For the most part this should be relatively safe for a player to do if they are simply miming punches and kicks as there would be no other performer on stage with them.

This said, I want to give the warning to any performers, directors and Emcees that this game does encourage stage combat, and it's worth discussing boundaries and limitations before rehearsing or performing this game. It can be easy for someone who isn't trained in stage combat to get caught up in the moment and risk injuring themselves or others.

Emcee Intro Script: Next up we're gonna play One Person Fight Club! In this game a single performer is going to create a scene where they play every character. Their challenge is to create multiple characters on their own, and then put them to war with each other in a spectacular display of stage combat.

Challenge Style: Solo scene/Stage Combat

Players: 1

Ask the audience for:

#1: A location.

#2: Something that may cause a dispute between people.

How to play the game:

#1: Don't talk about the movie that inspired this improv game...

#2: The performer should use the space they have available on the stage to establish an environment that features 2 or more characters in it.

#3: To perform as multiple characters the actor should ensure that every character has a distinct vocal quality and physical characteristics. The more different you can make them, the easier it will be for the audience to accept one performer as several different characters.

This can be achieved through things such as accent, tone of voice and vocabulary used for vocal work, and changing up the way the character holds themselves physically such as their style of walking and type of gestures they make.

#4: When swapping between characters you can use a technique known as 'a moment of suspension'. This is where the character you are playing freezes for a split second before you physically move to the stage position for the other character. Once there you then have a similar moment of suspension before continuing as the new character.

This will help show the audience that there is about to be a change and will allow the audience to get used to the different characters and their unique characteristics. The longer the scene goes on the more you can speed up the changes as the audience will quickly get used to the different voices and physicality if you have successfully made them distinct enough.

#5: Stage Combat. Once the scene has been established (1 to 2 minutes should be plenty), the performer can begin to escalate the scene to the point that the characters will have an elaborate Hollywood style action movie brawl. You will have to juggle playing both the attacking character and reacting as the character who has been hit.

A tip for achieving this is to use typical action movie quips and essentially narrate your way through the fight. For example:

Character 1: Hey you! How would you like a punch in the mouth?!

Character 2: Ouch! You split my lip! Hey lady, hand me that bottle!

Character 3: Here crack him over the head with this!

Character 2: Thanks! Take this!

Character 1: Ahhhh my head!

How does the game end? The whole game should only last between 2-3 minutes and ending it can be a judgement call made by the Emcee. A performer should build things up and can bring a scene to a natural conclusion where the fight ends either with a winner or with some kind of reconciliation.

Pro Tip #1: In terms of stage combat unless you're trained don't try doing anything elaborate. A fake punch to thin air is one thing, but there's no need to perform a backflip as if you've been thrown out a window.

Note: I won't go further into stage combat techniques in this book as it's a skillset in its own right, and I cannot possibly cover it in enough detail here to begin to give anyone a proper understanding of what goes into making staged fight scenes safe and effective. I will just say that if you play on the side of caution and stick to slapstick ideas, simple punches, kicks and stomps, miming weapons, and over the top reactions you should sail through this scene without risk of injury.

Pro Tip #2: Before performing this game in a show or a rehearsal you should do a physical warm up. This is good practice before doing any physical activity such as stage combat. A few stretches go a long way, and it's even worth doing a few stretches whilst the Emcee is getting suggestions from the audience for this very game. It will give the impression that you are gearing up for something exciting and will also help ready you if you've been sat for a while between games.

96: SIGN LANGUAGE

Emcee Intro Script: We're now going to play a game of Sign Language. One of our performers is going to give a speech, and another player is going to translate the speech into sign language...or their version of it anyway.

Challenge Style: Scene based/Physical

Players: 2+

Ask the audience for: A subject for the speaking character to do a presentation about.

Setup: The character giving the speech takes centre stage, whilst the player translating stands slightly to one side.

How to play the game:

#1: The speaking character gives a speech on the subject the audience has suggested.

#2: The character performing the sign language translates everything the speaking character says into a made-up sign language using over the top physicality and hand gestures.

How does the game end? As this game features a character giving a speech it should end with the character bringing the speech to a close.

Pro Tip #1: Whilst it is possible that the person giving the speech could play it for laughs, the game is designed more as a vehicle for the performer doing the sign language to interpret the speech in humorous ways. This doesn't mean the character speaking can't say any funny lines, but they are safe to play the scene strait-laced and let the character signing put funny twists on it.

Pro Tip #2: There is a rhythm to performing this game successfully that can be found through practice. The speaking character should allow enough breathing room for the audience to be able to take in what they have said, and also see how the signer has translated the speech into sign language. This doesn't mean the game is completely turn take, but the speaking character should give enough space around their sentences or ideas so that the audience can see how the sign language connects to their words.

SECTION 15: QUICK FIRE GAMES

These games are all about short, snappy scenes, one liners and puns. The quicker the wit, the better!

As the cowboy said to the artist…'draw'!

97: WORLD'S WORST

Emcee Intro Script: Our next game is World's Worst, in which our performers will perform short demonstrations of the world's worst examples of... various things that you suggest. Starting with the world's worst...

Challenge Style: Quick Fire/Pun based

Players: 1+

Ask the audience for: Things they would like to see examples of the world's worst.

Setup: The players stand on a back line or either side of the stage waiting to enter the space for their turn.

A bell or a buzzer may also be useful for the Emcee.

How to play the game:

#1: The Emcee calls out what the performers should provide examples of, such as the world's worst...plumber, or TV show host, or doctor.

#2: Players take turns to step forward to centre stage to show their idea for the world's worst example of that suggestion. They can do this solo, or with other players working together. Either way, the idea they show should only be a very short example. 5-10 seconds is plenty, and these examples are usually pun or single joke based ideas.

#3: If a player's idea doesn't get a big laugh or have an obvious end point the Emcee can buzz/ring a bell or call 'next' to move on to the next idea.

#4: The Emcee can periodically change the subject matter of the scenes by asking for another suggestion of the world's worst what?

How does the scene end? The Emcee should use their judgement of when the game has been played out enough and it is time to move on to something else.

Pro Tip #1: Try to keep your ideas short and snappy.

Pro Tip #2: Quick fire games are great for recurring gags, so look for opportunities to reference ideas that have already come up during the show.

98: CROSS THE ROAD

Emcee Intro Script: We're now going to play the Cross The Road joke game. The way this works is each of our performers will step forward and tell a joke based around the 'why did the chicken cross the road?' joke. But in this game, we will replace the chicken with something of your choosing.

Challenge Style: Joke telling/Pun based

Players: 1+

Ask the audience for: A profession, animal, or group of people (such as jocks, nerds, teens.)

How to play the game:

#1: The performers have to finish the punchlines of the joke in this format:

Why did the *(audience suggestion)* cross the road? *(And then make up a punchline)*

How does the game end? The Emcee ends the game at their discretion.

Pro Tip #1: Try to find connections between the audience suggestion and the idea of crossing the road.

For example, if the audience suggests 'a tiger' you could say something like:

Why did the tiger cross the road? Because it was trying to eat the zebra crossing.

This plays on the idea that a big cat would eat a zebra and that a zebra crossing is a type of road crossing in the UK.

99: 99 BLANKS WALK INTO A BAR

Emcee Intro Script: We're now going to play 99 Blanks. The way this works is each of our performers will step forward and tell a joke that begins with 99 'blanks' walk into a bar...and then they will finish the joke based around what you have suggested the blank should be.

Challenge Style: Joke telling/Pun based

Players: 1+

Ask the audience for: A profession, object or animal.

How to play the game:

#1: The players in the game stand along the back line of the stage and step forwards one at a time when they have a joke to tell.

#2: Players have to tell a joke where the punchline relates back to the audience suggestion.

#3: All the jokes told follows this format:

99 *(Audience suggestion)* walk into a bar and...*(punchline)*

For example if the audience suggested 'Dentists' as the subject here are a few jokes performers could say:

- 99 dentists walk into a bar and the barman says: You're here a bit early. We don't open until 'tooth hurty'.
- 99 dental nurses walk into a bar and when the barman asks where the dentists are, they say we're filling in.
- 99 dentists walk into a bar, and asks is this disco night? Cause we're here to floss *(This can be followed by doing the floss dance move)*

#4: The Emcee can regularly change the subject of the jokes being told by asking the audience for more suggestions.

How does the game end? The Emcee can decide when enough jokes have been told.

Pro Tip #1: These don't have to be the greatest jokes of all time. Any kind of play on words or silly idea should suffice to get a laugh or a groan out of the audience. If you fail to get either the Emcee can break the moment by calling 'Next'.

100: SCENES FROM THE AUDIENCE

Emcee Intro Script: Next up we're going to play Scenes From The Audience! Before the show we asked the audience to write down ideas for scenes they'd like the performers to create, and we're going to go through a bunch of them now in quickfire rounds!

Challenge Style: Pun based/Quick fire

Players: 2+

Ask the audience for: To write down ideas for scenes. This will need to be done in advance of the game. Ideally this could be at the start of the show, and then you gather their suggestions during an interval.

Setup: Ask the audience to write ideas for scenes they'd like the performers to create on slips of paper that will be used later in the show. You'll need to provide the audience with pens/paper to be able to do this.

On the stage, all the performers stand along a backline or at the sides of the stage ready to step forward and enter the scene.

How to play the game:

#1: The Emcee reads aloud the idea/name of the scene that the audience suggested.

#2: One or more players can step forwards to create a short scene based on the idea.

#3: Once we have an idea of the scene, or the player has got a laugh the Emcee can call 'Next' or press a bell/buzzer to indicate it's time to move on.

#4: You can get multiple interpretations and versions of the same scene idea. The Emcee should only move on to a new scene suggestion once it seems like the performers have run out of ideas for the current scene.

How does the game end? The Emcee calls for the end of the game once several different scene ideas have been done by the performers, and it feels right to move on to something else in the show.

Pro Tip #1: Keep your scenes short. The expectation with this game is for scenes to last 1-5 sentences at most. Often a pun or silly interpretation of the theme is all you need.

Pro Tip #2: Reincorporation. With this game you can use running gags to great effect. If you have the opportunity to revisit a joke from a previous scene with a new twist on it this will often get a good laugh.

Likewise, this game is a great opportunity to revisit scenes and characters from previous games you may have performed elsewhere in the overall show.

101: PROPS

Emcee Intro Script: Our next game is called Props. In a game of props our improvisers will have some interesting props which they have to reinterpret in as many different ways as they can think of in some quick fire scenes.

Challenge Style: Quick fire/Pun based

Players: 4

Ask the audience for: N/A. Nothing in this game.

Setup: Each pair of two players are provided with an interesting prop/props and given half the stage each as their performance area. The Emcee can use a buzzer or call 'Next' to move the focus from one team to another.

How to play the game:

#1: Players have to come up with as many different ways to interpret the props they are working with as possible.

#2: Each team is given around 5 seconds to show off their interpretation of the props before the Emcee switches focus to the other pair.

How does the game end?

The Emcee uses their judgement of when the performers are running out of new ideas for how to interpret the props.

Pro Tip #1: You will want to come up with as many creative ways for reinterpreting the props as possible. This will require thinking outside the box and using your imagination to help the audience to see the same prop over and over again as different things in their minds eye. Here are some examples:

If a team has a generic circular shape it could be interpreted in many ways. Here are a few ideas of how a circle could be used:

- As a steering wheel of a car.
- As a wheel on a car that one player is having to change.
- As a dinner plate.
- Held up as if it is the Sun/Moon/a planet in the sky.
- As a 2D soccer ball.

- As a frisbee.
- A giant tablet that will be hard to swallow.

As a second example if a team had long stick like objects to use they could be interpreted in the following ways:

- A sword.
- A light sabre.
- A broom/mop.
- A flagpole missing the flag.
- The world's longest hot dog.

102: ANIMATED GIFS

Emcee Intro Script: In Animated Gifs, solo players or teams will compete to make short 1-5 second scenes mimicking memes and animated gifs like you'd find on the internet.

Challenge Style: Physical Theatre/Quick fire

Players: 2-8 (Either solos, or split into teams)

Ask the audience for: Terms you'd search for when looking for an animated gif or memes on the internet.

How to play the game:

#1: Make short 1-5 second scenes based on audience suggestions.

#2: You can use words/sounds in place of captions, but ideally these should work as silent scenes that fit the audience suggestion.

#3: The scenes can be played once or performed in a continuous loop to mimic how animated gifs will play on loop.

How does the game end?

This game ends when the Emcee judges that enough ideas have been performed and it is time to move on.

Pro Tip #1: If playing a gif scene in a loop, you could slightly heighten your expressions/voice in each repetitions for added effect, but this is a fine line to cross as too many alterations will lose the effect of your performance being in the style of a looping animated gif.

SECTION 16: DUB STEP IT UP

No, I'm afraid this isn't about the music genre 'dubstep'. Instead, this is the section on games where players have to provide voice overs, vocal sound effects and translate languages like a voice over artist.

Dubbing can double your fun!

103: FILM DUB

Emcee Intro Script: Next up, we're going to play Film Dub. In this game our improvisers will provide a new voice track for a piece of film that we are going to play without the sound on.

Challenge Style: Voiceover

Players: 1+

Ask the audience for: N/A

Setup: For this game you will need a screen or projection so that both the audience and the players can see footage that they will be dubbing. This will need to be a reasonable size so that everyone can see it clearly...so don't try playing this game in a big theatre if you're trying to watch a clip on a phone!

A note about copyright: It may sound a great idea to use a clip from films like Harry Potter or The Avengers for this game, but as those are still under copyright at the time of writing (I can't imagine people will still be reading this book by the time they are no longer in copyright) it would almost certainly break copyright laws.

There may be loopholes of things being fair use or transformative, but I'm not sure they'd be worth the hassle for the purposes of this game. Check the laws of your country in regard to this and make your own choices based on this information. You have been warned.

The good news is that there are thousands of hours of old films that are no longer in copyright which would be perfect for this game. Research public domain films and films that are old enough to have had their copyrights expire and you'll find loads.

How to play the game:

#1: Footage is played without sound for both the players and the audience to watch. The footage should include characters who talk.

#2: Players provide voiceovers to the footage as if they are the characters speaking. This should attempt to be in sync with the character's mouths moving, but shouldn't try to replicate what is being said in the original soundtrack. When the character on screen moves their mouth, you can provide a voice for them and when they stop you stop.

How does the game end? This game ends when the scene in the footage ends. Ideally this will only be a 1-3 minute clip. If you are really daring, it is possible to play this game with an entire film if you choose to.

Pro Tip #1: With this game you can completely change the story of the footage you are dubbing over. This said, keep in mind that the footage is the footage and will not change to fit your new narrative. If you dub a character as saying: 'I'm going to kill you' and then the character on screen doesn't kill another character you will have to adapt your next lines to reflect this.

Pro tips #2: This game gives you a great opportunity to point out things in the footage that may be funny or obscure observations about it. Is the wallpaper in the scene ugly? Or does a character have an odd expression on their face? If so, make the character you are dubbing comment on it. The audience will find this kind of thing funny as it will be obvious this was not what was said in the original soundtrack of the film.

104: FOREIGN FILM DUB

Emcee Intro Script: The next game is called Foreign Film Dub. In it two players will perform a scene in a gibberish language, and another two players will provide a translation of what the gibberish language means.

Challenge Style: Scene based

Players: 4

Ask the audience for:

#1: A real foreign language.

#2: A scenario such as something that may happen in a soap opera.

Setup: Two players stand on stage, whilst another two players stand on each side of the stage as translators.

How to play the game:

#1: Players 1 and 2 perform a scene where they can only speak in a nonsense gibberish version of a foreign language.

For clarity we will refer to the final two players as Translator 1 and Translator 2. Translator 1 translates for Player 1 and Translator 2 translates for Player 2.

#2: The rhythm this game takes is that every gibberish line said must be translated before another gibberish line can be said.

For Example:

Player 1: Dobble baba wazz yip rilipa.

Translator 1: I love your new hairdo!

Player 2: Guld. O frinolt. Machee da boojapop.

Translator 2: Thanks. I always wanted to look like a skunk!

If you don't follow this pattern and both gibberish speaking players say lines without translation in between, it will become confusing for when the translators should speak. Likewise, if a translator speaks before the gibberish player has spoken it would confuse the audience as to what they are translating.

How does the game end? This game ends at the Emcee's discretion.

Pro Tip #1: Some people will play this as if the translators are part of the scene, and therefore the gibberish speaking players can acknowledge and interact with them. I find this game is best played where the gibberish speaking players simply ignore their translators, as it lacks logic that the characters both speaking the same gibberish language would need each other translated.

Pro Tip #2: If you are a translator you can have fun with your translation. An example would include playing against the gibberish player's intention. So, if the gibberish player says something with a lot of excitement you could translate it to be something you wouldn't expect them to be excited about.

Another example would be to contrast the length of the translation to the length of the gibberish line. For example, if the gibberish speaking player says a line that sounds 10-15 words long and you translate it as 'Yes.' It will usually get a laugh. The reverse of this is also true, so if a gibberish speaking player just says a small amount and you translate it into a monologue.

Pro Tip #3: If you are one of the gibberish speaking players stay in the moment whilst the gibberish is being translated. Don't just stand there as if you are waiting for the translation to happen. Listen and show the emotion of what is being said to keep the energy of the scene up.

105: SOUND FX

Emcee Intro Script: Our next game is called Sound FX and the way it works is that one of our performers will create a scene physically, and another performer will use a microphone to create sound effects for what that player is doing.

Challenge Style: Physical/Voice Over

Players: 2

Ask the audience for: A scenario such as where you might go in a hurry.

Set Up: The player providing sound effects will need a microphone, and to stand to the side or just off stage.

How to play the game:

#1: Player 1 creates a scene physically but does not speak or make any sounds themselves.

#2: Player 2 uses the microphone to create sound effects to compliment what Player 1 is doing physically in the scene.

#3: Generally speaking, the scene shouldn't involve speech from either player. The focus should be on sound effects and not dubbing and lip syncing each other.

#4: Player 1 should only play one character and not try to play multiple characters as this will get confusing. If Player 1 meets other characters in the scene, they should mime reacting to them, and Player 2 should provide sound effects to suggest other characters are there.

How does the game end? Either when the scene reaches a natural conclusion, or the Emcee deems it has gone on long enough.

Pro Tip #1: In this game there shouldn't be one player always leading the other. It shouldn't be that Player 2 only provides a sound effect if Player 1 does something. Nor should it be that Player 1 only does something if Player 2 makes a sound effect. For best results both should happen.

If Player 1 does an action Player 2 should provide a sound effect for it. If Player 2 does a random or unexpected sound effect Player 1 should react to it.

Pro Tip #2: Think about what things can make sounds and try to incorporate them into the scene.

Ideas and examples of things that make sound effects:

Footsteps, Breathing, Screams, Sneezes, Grunts, Thunder, Doors, Wind, Punches, Farts, Door Bells, Fire alarms, Vehicles, Animals, Clocks, Telephones, Computers, Rain, Toilets, Instruments, Ghosts, Magic, Chewing, Stomachs, Claps, Radios, TV, Kisses, Cartoon FX, Crying

XII: AFTERWORD

And scene! Wow! Is this the end of the book? Really? I don't know what is the bigger surprise to me – that I've actually written this whole book, or that I've managed to hold your attention long enough that you've actually read it through to the end!?!?!

I had no idea when I first sat down to start writing this book what an adventure it was going to be for me. That may sound like a typical eye roll inducing thing for a writer to say, but I mean it quite literally. This has been an adventure. To compile this book, I've really had to break down and examine each of these games in a depth that I've never thought about before. This has often resulted in me playing the games by myself at 2am, performing as multiple characters and creating scenes featuring fire breathing dragons, alien xenomorphs and performing open heart surgery!

Sometimes I'd film these scenes so I could watch them back and really pick apart the process. As you can imagine these clips can be bonkers to watch as I play solo versions of Stand Sit Bend, or a Gemini Scene, whilst also fulfilling the duties of Emcee and audience members. Whether these all truly helped me write the book is hard to say, but they certainly have given me a good basis for my upcoming one man Extreme Improv show!

Oh, and to answer the question of what is the thing that the title of Section 11, 'Who Goes There?' refers to? The clue was in the question... 'The Thing' is the answer, which is a movie directed by John Carpenter and starring Kurt Russell. It's one of my favourite movies, and is based on a novella called Who Goes There? by John W. Campbell Jr...so yeah...mystery solved. This may seem a weird inclusion in the wrap up at the end of my book, but what the hey, it's my book, and by this stage of writing it I'm more than a little giddy with the process. Also, it's 3am, and this seemed a brilliant idea to entice readers to finish to the end to find the answer to the question...did it work? Moving on...

I really hope that you've found this book useful, and that it's given you lots of helpful insights into how the many improv games work. A long time ago I realised that there are the rules you tell the audience so they get an idea of what you're doing, and then there are loads more almost secret rules which if you know can elevate a scene from being just ok, to being absolutely amazing! If any of my tips or thoughts in this book help you to create better scenes, feel more at ease with how to play the games and give both you and your audience a more enjoyable time I'll feel I've done a good job.

As I said at the start of the book, my personal number one rule in improv is to do all you can to make each show fun for the audience and yourself. If you have fun and emit a positive light in the room, your audience will have fun and fill your space with laughter. After a show I am usually buzzing with energy and can't sleep as I'm already thinking about the next show or creating a new game that popped into my head when on stage earlier that night.

I've massively enjoyed writing this book and am already compiling a list of games for a follow up book. This will include dozens more classic games which I've not covered yet, and a bunch of new creations I've been working on which I haven't quite tinkered with enough yet to iron out all the bugs. I've always taken great pride and pleasure in creating and developing new improv games, and I'm always excited when I get to teach a new game to a performer or student. Some of them are really wacky so I may need a few crash test dummies before I can unleash them on the world!

So, until next time, keep playing, laugh loads and stay Extreme!

XIII: ACKNOWLEDGMENTS

The first thank you I'd like to give is to my lovely girlfriend Rachel. The first Extreme Improv show you came to was poorly lit, in a random venue in a dodgy part of London and had a total audience of less than 10. As far as first impressions of what I do go, it couldn't have been much worse!

You have joined me on the Extreme Improv journey with me across the UK, and on all our journeys abroad. Thank you for taking photos of the shows and flyering with me, and for allowing me to convince you to join me on stage. I'd especially like to thank you for all your hours proofreading every page of this book. You gave me fantastic and insightful feedback for my writing and made me realise that I really don't know the difference between 'then' and 'than'.

My next thanks go to my family. My parents Jane and Philip, who have always been there for me, and supported me pursuing my ridiculous dreams. I want to thank you for every play you've come to watch, every lift I've had to a rehearsal, every costume that I've needed making the day before a show, for helping proofread this book and for telling me not to give up and to keep trying when I've been down.

I'd also like to thank my sisters Eve and Sarah. As my older siblings, not only have you both been there since day 1, but you have also both supported me since day 1. You were both there when I had a little hurt swim, and have heard me talk nonsense my whole life. You have both let me stay at your homes so I could follow improv opportunities and have both also spent time looking through this book to give me feedback. I especially want to thank Eve for her inventive colour coded feedback system which allowed me to know how I'd gone wrong before I'd even read the words!

Next, I'd like to thank my niece Sophie, who may be a bit too young to read this book at the time of writing, but who I look forward to teaching all of these games to. Also I think it's pretty cool to thank a baby in an acknowledgments section, so thank you Sophie for being a baby so I could do this.

And if I've thanked a baby, I may as well go all in and thank my pets...because why not?! Firstly, I'd like to thank Sparky and Buddy, my budgie and King Charles Cavalier Spaniel respectively. I named my theatre company Sparky

Buddy Productions after you both, and you're just awesome. Buddy in particular has been true to his name as my best Buddy, and I involve him in Extreme Improv at every opportunity I can.

And also, thanks to Chunky, Holly, Lucy and Tiny who were all incredible King Charles Cavalier Spaniels, Freddie, Ellie, Micky, Nipper, Ozzie, Ausie and Magic, who along with Sparky were amazing feathered friends when I was growing up. Thanks to Poorly and the other hundreds of stick insects, sea monkeys and aqua dragons I have had, and also to my rodent pals: Rusty, Toffee, Dusty, Sandy, April, Toaster, Mrs, Super B, and Bingo Baby He-Man who was my first ever pet.

I'd like to thank my pre-Extreme Improv ImproDigies cast mates for joining me for my first improv shows.

In terms of Extreme Improv cast I'd like to thank Adam, Angus, Paul, Vicky, Romy, Paul, Annie, Aaron, and Rebecca for being the first cast to play on stage and compete for the Extreme Improv Championship. Thank you all for showing trust in my ideas and being super funny and brave on stage in the 2017 Camden Fringe and beyond.

Thank you to James, Ellie, Sam, Tom, Sean, Vicky, Adam, Ione, Miranda, Rebecca, Michael, Haydn, Hazel, Bez, Aston, Holly, Jae, Matt, Tara and everyone else who has joined us on stage multiple times. Also to all our guest performers who have only been on stage with us once or twice (so far). You've all been great friends, and excellent and hilarious improvisers.

In recent times I've had the pleasure to meet and perform with so many more great improvisers through our Radio Rumble Podcast show, and the XStreamed virtual shows. Many of you I've yet to meet in real life, and look forward to doing so, but big shout outs to Dave, Lottie, Molly, Ned, Ashara, Al, Ruth, Diz, Shellyta, Beth, Mac, Danny, Sarah, Allan, Andrew, Assad, J, Claire, JJ, Lusy, Nick, Max, Hannah, Elke, Damian, Rahmeen, Ashley, Chris, Mike, Chad, Emma, Deirdre, PJ and Steve.

I must also thank my imaginary friends. There are too many of you to list here, but you know who you are.

Lastly, I'd like to thank everyone who has supported Extreme Improv over the years. Every audience member who has laughed and clapped and enjoyed the show. I'd like to thank every festival organiser and venue manager who has been kind and welcoming to Extreme Improv around the globe. Your continued support means the world to me, and I look forward to bringing Extreme Improv to more venues, countries and audiences.

Thank you to everyone who has supported Extreme Improv!

CPSIA information can be obtained
at www.ICGtesting.com
Printed in the USA
LVHW102124100922
728089LV00004B/170